Women and American Politics

Critical Topics in American Government Series

Voice of the People: Elections and Voting in the United States
Alan Abramowitz

Women and American Politics: The Challenges of Political Leadership
Lori Cox Han

Organized Interests and American Government
David Lowery and Holly Brasher

Understanding the U.S. Supreme Court: Cases and Controversies
Kevin McGuire

Campaigns in the 21st Century
Richard Semiatin

Women and American Politics

The Challenges of Political Leadership

Lori Cox Han

Chapman University

Boston   Burr Ridge, IL   Dubuque, IA   Madison, WI   New York
San Francisco   St. Louis   Bangkok   Bogotá   Caracas   Kuala Lumpur
Lisbon   London   Madrid   Mexico City   Milan   Montreal   New Delhi
Santiago   Seoul   Singapore   Sydney   Taipei   Toronto

Higher Education

WOMEN AND AMERICAN POLITICS: THE CHALLENGES OF POLITICAL LEADERSHIP

Published by McGraw-Hill, a business unit of The McGraw-Hill Companies, Inc., 1221 Avenue of the Americas, New York, NY, 10020. Copyright © 2007 by The McGraw-Hill Companies, Inc. All rights reserved. No part of this publication may be reproduced or distributed in any form or by any means, or stored in a database or retrieval system, without the prior written consent of The McGraw-Hill Companies, Inc., including, but not limited to, in any network or other electronic storage or transmission, or broadcast for distance learning.

Some ancillaries, including electronic and print components, may not be available to customers outside the United States.

This book is printed on acid-free paper.

1 2 3 4 5 6 7 8 9 0 DOC/DOC 0 9 8 7 6 5

ISBN: 0-07-293077-2
ISBN: 978-0-07-293077-1

Editor in Chief: *Emily Barrosse*
Publisher: *Lyn Uhl*
Senior Sponsoring Editor: *Monica Eckman*
Developmental Editor: *Kate Scheinman*
Marketing Manager: *Katherine Bates*
Managing Editor: *Jean Dal Porto*
Project Manager: *Jean R. Starr*
Art Director: *Jeanne Schreiber*
Design Manager: *Laurie J. Entringer*
Senior Photo Research Coordinator: *Alexandra Ambrose*
Cover Credit: © *Manuel Balce Ceneta/AP/Wide World Photos*
Production Supervisor: *Jason I. Huls*
Composition: *10/12 Palatino, International Typesetting & Composition*
Printing: *45# New Era Matte Plus, R.R. Donnelley/Crawfordsville*

Library of Congress Cataloging-in-Publication Data
Han, Lori Cox.
    Women and American politics : the challenges of political leadership / Lori Cox Han.
        p. cm.
    Includes bibliographical references and index.
    ISBN 0-07-293077-2 (softcover : alk. paper)
    ISBN 978-0-07-293077-1
    1. Women in politics—United States. 2. Political leadership—United States. I. Title.
HQ1236.5.U6H34 2007
320'.082'0973—dc22   2005052277

The Internet addresses listed in the text were accurate at the time of publication. The inclusion of a website does not indicate an endorsement by the authors of McGraw-Hill, and McGraw-Hill does not guarantee the accuracy of the information presented at these sites.

www.mhhe.com

For my daughter Taylor Ann,
and all the other future women leaders of her generation

About the Author

LORI COX HAN is professor and chair of political science at Chapman University in Orange, California. She received her PhD in political science at the University of Southern California in 1997 and specializes in the American presidency, mass media and politics, and women and politics. She is the author of *Governing From Center Stage: White House Communication Strategies During the Television Age of Politics* and co-editor of *In the Public Domain: Presidents and the Challenge of Public Leadership* (with Diane J. Heith). Her research has also appeared in *Presidential Studies Quarterly, Congress and the Presidency,* and *White House Studies.*

Contents

Preface   *ix*

Chapter 1 Women and Political Leadership   1

Women as Political Leaders: A Historical Perspective   2
Women as Political Leaders: Does Gender Matter?   4
Plan of the Book   9

Chapter 2 The Women's Movement and Feminism in the
United States   15

The First Wave of the Women's Movement in America   16
The Second Wave: The Modern Women's Movement   24
The Third Wave: Generation X and Beyond   29
Feminisms and American Politics   31
Conclusion   35

Chapter 3 Women as Political Participants   40

Women and Political Socialization   41
Women and the Mass Media   43
Women as Voters   47
Women in Political Parties and Interest Groups   51
Conclusion   57

Chapter 4 Women as Political Candidates   62

Recruiting Women Candidates   63
Women Candidates and the Electoral Process   66
Media Coverage of Women Candidates   70
Conclusion   75

Chapter 5 Women as Legislators   80

Women and Legislative Leadership   81
Women in Congress: A History   82
Women in Congress: The Policy Agenda   90
Women in State Legislatures   94
Conclusion   98

Chapter 6 Women and Executive Leadership   102

Executive Leadership from a Woman's Perspective   103
A Woman President   106
Women in the Executive Branch   112
Governors and Other Statewide Positions   118
Mayors   120
Conclusion   122

Chapter 7 Women in the Judiciary   128

Women and the Law   129
Women and the Legal Profession   131
Women as Federal Judges   133
Women, the Courts, and the Policy Agenda   138
Women as State and Local Judges   139
Do Women Judges Act Differently?   142
Conclusion   143

Chapter 8 Conclusion: Women and Political Leadership
        in the Twenty-first Century   148

The Women's Movement   149
Voting Trends and the Gender Gap   150
Women as Candidates   151
Women as Officeholders   152
Conclusion: Women and Leadership Revisited   154

INDEX   I–1

Preface

Political leadership is always a dominant theme throughout my women and politics course, as well as many of my other courses. Leadership in and of itself is a fascinating topic for political scientists as we seek to better understand the unique dynamics of this concept, not only in how such a malleable term should be defined, but what role, if any, it plays in shaping our governing institutions. This text attempts to capture that theme in a way that will interest and engage students, both female and male, to better understand the role that women have played and are currently playing in the American political process. It explores whether their presence has brought any significant changes in public policies or how our governing institutions operate. The areas and themes included in this book provide the essential broader topics for teaching a women and politics course from a political science perspective, while also considering the issue of women's leadership as a core theme and mode of analysis as more women get elected to office (Congress and state governors), appointed to high-ranking federal positions (the executive and judicial branches), and as the United States moves closer to electing the first woman president (a timely topic as the 2008 presidential campaign draws closer). The design of the book, by topic, is similar to many introductory American government texts. The first half of the book deals mostly with mass politics, after an appropriate historical perspective, followed by the second half of the book, which covers political institutions. Therefore, the book lends itself to providing students with a gendered look at key topics in American government, and is intended not only for courses that specifically consider women in politics but many other American government courses as well.

There are several areas of research in a variety of disciplines focusing on women, gender, and feminism, and many of them intersect with a discussion of women in American politics. My goal in writing this book was to provide an interesting, lively, and timely discussion of contemporary political issues in America that involve women as political participants, candidates, and office holders, as well as to make this book readable and accessible to students of all levels. It is also my hope that I have provided just enough of a historical context to get students interested in the evolution of women in American political life to seek more information and knowledge on this important topic. I highly recommend readers take a look at the many wonderful works that I have included in the Suggested Readings sections at the end of every chapter except the last, and to keep in mind that these suggestions are only a start to the fascinating and creative scholarship that is now available to readers on this and related topics. The study of women and politics has emerged as a powerful voice within the discipline of political science in the last few decades, and I hope that readers find this text a useful addition to the ongoing dialogue.

As with any book project, large or small, there are many people to acknowledge and thank. First and foremost, I want to thank Monica Eckman, who first approached me about the possibility of writing a women and politics text for McGraw-Hill in the spring of 2002. This type of project was nowhere on my research agenda at the time, but the combination of Monica's enthusiasm for the book and my own long-term interest in the topic convinced me to seize the opportunity. In addition, my developmental editor on the project, Kate Scheinman, has provided tremendous support and encouragement along the way. With both Monica and Kate backing me at every step of the project, I could not have asked for a better editorial team.

I am also indebted to the many reviewers who read various drafts and versions of chapters, as well as the last round of reviewers who read the entire manuscript: Jilda M. Aliotta, University of Hartford; Lisa Baldez, Dartmouth College; Janet K. Boles, Marquette University; Marla Brettschneider, University of New Hampshire; Dianne Bystrom, Iowa State University; Stefanie A. Chambers, Trinity College; Kathleen Dolan, University of Wisconsin Milwaukee; Daryl R. Fair, The College of New Jersey; Joyce Gelb, City University of New York; Ann Gordon, Ohio University; Marsha Matson, University of Miami; Richard D. Shingles, Virginia Tech; Kendra Stewart, Eastern Kentucky University; Robert P. Watson, Florida Atlantic University; Donald E. Whistler, University of Central Arkansas; and Laura R. Woliver, University of South Carolina. The comments and thoughtful suggestions I received not only broadened my perspective on the topic, but also helped make the book stronger. The reviews also saved me from including a few factual errors, although any that remain are my sole responsibility.

I would also like to acknowledge several colleagues who provided assistance, advice, and support throughout the writing and editing process of this book. I am grateful to Ann Gordon at Ohio University for her friendship and for always allowing me to rely on her expertise on women and politics when I needed to hear feedback that I could trust. Michael Genovese at Loyola Marymount University has been a terrific friend and mentor, and has helped foster my growing interest in leadership studies. I would also like to thank two of my former colleagues at Austin College: Bernice Melvin, for always lending an ear and providing insight and advice from someone who had already been through the trenches before I arrived; and Jerry Johnson, who agreed to read a few early drafts of chapters, and for all the articles on women and corporate leadership that he provided, free of charge, in his role as my "trusty research assistant." Finally, I want to thank my husband Tom for his never-ending love and support, and for all the times he took the kids out of the house so that I could spend some quality time in front of the computer; and Taylor and Davis, for their continued patience and cooperation (most of the time) while I was working on this project.

Lori Cox Han
Chapman University

CHAPTER 1

Women and Political Leadership

The only safe ship in a storm is leadership.

—Faye Wattleton
president of the Center for the Advancement of Women

*I*magine that politics in Washington, DC, as you know it is about to change dramatically. By the time you wake up tomorrow morning, the political landscape will have changed so much that nothing about our system of government will ever be the same. This massive political shakeup that will occur within the United States government will make it difficult to even comprehend the impact on how Americans view their national leaders, as well as how the government will operate on a day-to-day basis. This news will be so shocking that the entire world will watch in awe and disbelief. What change in our national government could be so radical? Imagine that every position of political leadership, whether elected or appointed, were suddenly held by a woman—not only the president, but all of the cabinet positions and her close advisors, all of the leadership positions within the Congress (including the Speaker of the House and the senate majority leader), and all nine members of the U.S. Supreme Court. In addition, every state governor is now a woman, as is every leadership position in each of the 50 state legislatures, as well as every mayoral position in every city across the country.

While theoretically this kind of extreme shift in political leadership is possible, it is probably unlikely. American women, who have had the right to vote only since 1920, are still struggling to reach parity with their male counterparts in political leadership positions, let alone dominating the entire political system. In theory, democratically elected political bodies should look something like the larger society that they represent. This provides legitimacy to political institutions, particularly in regard to women, who make up slightly more than half of the U. S. population. However, thinking about such an extreme shift in the political landscape is quite instructive, since it was not that many years ago that men held every political leadership position in Washington, DC. The thought of every position of power being held by a woman raises an interesting question—does gender matter when electing political leaders? Perhaps more important, how do Americans view women as political leaders, and does this impact their chance of success within the political arena? In a political age so driven by the influence of the news media, do negative stereotypes about women as political officeholders and powerbrokers harm their career opportunities in the public sector? These questions are crucial when studying the role of women in American politics because not only do women have the right as citizens to full political participation (not only as voters but as officeholders as well), their participation has an impact on the political process and on the outcome of public policy debates.

WOMEN AS POLITICAL LEADERS: A HISTORICAL PERSPECTIVE

According to political scientist Barbara Kellerman, while few women have held formal positions of authority throughout world history, that is "not tantamount to saying they did not exercise power or exert influence."[1] However, the traditional view of politics suggests that those with political power are those who hold specific leadership positions within government. From that vantage point, how have American women fared?

Within the executive branch, no woman has ever been elected president or vice president, while only two women have ever served as secretary of state (Madeleine Albright and Condoleezza Rice) and one as attorney general (Janet Reno). These two cabinet positions, along with secretary of defense and secretary of the treasury, are considered the most prominent cabinet positions among the now 15 cabinet-level departments in the executive branch. The two most recent presidents made these three appointments—with Albright and Reno serving in Bill Clinton's administration and Rice serving in George W. Bush's administration—which means that this has been a fairly new trend. The early cabinet appointments of Frances Perkins by Franklin Roosevelt in 1933 (as secretary of labor) and Oveta Culp Hobby by

Dwight Eisenhower in 1953 (as secretary of health, education, and welfare, which is now split between the two departments of Health and Human Services and Education) are considered political anomalies; the next woman to be appointed to a cabinet position would not come until 1975 when Gerald Ford selected Carla Anderson Hills as secretary of housing and urban development. In total, 30 women have held 35 cabinet or cabinet-level positions (including the positions of United Nations ambassador, national security advisor, special/U.S. trade representative, director of the Office of Management and Budget, chair of the Council of Economic Advisors, administrator of the Environmental Protection Agency, administrator of the Small Business Administration, and director of the Office of Personnel Management) since 1933.

Special advisors within the White House are often considered even more powerful and influential than cabinet appointments. No woman has ever served as a chief of staff, and only one woman has served as a presidential press secretary (Dee Dee Myers served as Clinton's press secretary from 1993 to 1994) and as the national security advisor (Condoleezza Rice served in this role, considered a cabinet-level appointment, during George W. Bush's first term from 2001 to 2005). Karen Hughes, who held the joint title of director of communications and counselor to the president for George W. Bush from 2001 until her resignation in 2003, is considered one of the most influential women to ever serve in an advisory capacity to a president within the Oval Office.

In the judicial branch, only two women have ever served on the U.S. Supreme Court (Sandra Day O'Connor, nominated by Ronald Reagan in 1981, and Ruth Bader Ginsburg, nominated by Bill Clinton in 1993). In the legislative branch, no woman had ever held a top leadership position until Nancy Pelosi's (D-CA) ascent in 2003 to Democratic minority leader in the House of Representatives. At the state level, only 28 women have ever served as governor, and Ella Grasso's (D) election as governor of Connecticut in 1975 marked the first time that a woman was elected to the top state executive position in her own right, without replacing her husband in office (due either to his death or his inability to succeed himself).

Since the days of Nellie Tayloe Ross (D-WY) and Miriam "Ma" Ferguson (D-TX), both elected in 1925 as governor of their respective states to succeed their husbands, and since Frances Perkins made history as the first woman cabinet member in Washington, women have made tremendous progress, at least statistically, in gaining access to elective or appointed office at most levels of government. Yet reaching a level of parity that is representative of the population at large, in which women voters slightly outnumber male voters, is still many decades away. Due to recent gains for women in elected positions, public perceptions seem to indicate that most Americans believe that women are receiving equal treatment in regard to leadership opportunities in both the public and private sector. According to the Center for American Women and Politics, as of 2005 there are now more women serving in the U.S. Congress than ever before—14 in the Senate and 66 in the House of Representatives. In addition, a total of 81 women hold statewide executive positions, 1,663 women serve as state legislators, and 14 women serve as mayors of the 100 largest U.S. cities.

As impressive as those numbers may be, however, the percentages tell a different story. Of the 535 seats in the U.S. Congress, women hold only 15 percent of those. In statewide executive positions, such as governors, lieutenant governors, and attorney generals, only 25.1 percent are held by women (and only 8 of 50 governors are women). A total of 22.5 percent of state legislators are women, and those 14 large-city mayors represent only 14 percent of the 100 largest cities in the nation (topping the list is Mayor Laura Miller of Dallas, which ranks as the 9th largest city in the nation, followed by Mayor Jane Campbell of Cleveland, Ohio, which then drops down to 35th in the ranking of cities by population). Although women have made tremendous progress in gaining access to positions of political leadership in recent years, they are still "underrepresented at the top and overrepresented at the bottom" in American government at all levels.[2] According to political scientist Susan C. Bourque, public perceptions of women as active participants in the political process have broadened, yet various factors of American life continue to restrict political leadership opportunities for women. They include sexual division of labor (women are still predominantly responsible for child care and household chores); work structures and sex role expectations (lack of "flex-time" and other career advancement opportunities for women with family responsibilities); ambivalence about women exercising power; and perpetual issues such as how the media can portray women leaders in a negative light.[3]

WOMEN AS POLITICAL LEADERS: DOES GENDER MATTER?

Defining the term leadership and how it applies to the American political process is an essential aspect in understanding the unique dynamics within democratic governing institutions. As women continue to gain more prominence as active participants in the American political and electoral process as voters, candidates, and officeholders, it becomes even more important to understand how leadership is defined from a woman's perspective. The essential question becomes, do women political leaders make a difference in their style, approach, and impact to governing and policymaking? And, perhaps just as important, how do women differ from each other in leadership positions?

In general terms, *leadership* is defined as the ability to encourage, influence, or inspire others to act in pursuit of a common goal or agenda. Defining such a malleable term like *leadership*, however, is not an easy task. Leadership theories abound that discuss specific traits, skills, styles, or personality characteristics that leaders possess, or certain situations that emerge to allow leaders to act accordingly.[4] Perhaps one of the most widely recognized theories of leadership is the work of James MacGregor Burns, who introduced the idea of transformational leadership in the late 1970s.[5] For Burns, leadership is more than just the act of wielding power; it involves the relationship between leaders and followers. Burns states that transactional leadership refers to what most leaders are able to accomplish—the day-to-day exchanges between leaders and followers that have come to be expected. For example, a congressional candidate may promise to introduce a bill to reform the nation's health care system, and once elected, he or she follows through with that plan. Transformational leadership, on the other hand, provides more than just a simple change to a particular policy. A transformational leader provides broader changes to the entire political system that raise the level of motivation and morality in both the leader and the follower. As Burns states, "transforming leaders define public values that embrace the supreme and enduring principles of a people."[6]

However, as Burns and many other scholars have pointed out in recent years, the definition of *leadership* is fluid—it can change based on the context and situation in which the term is used. While a universal and precise definition of *effective* or *successful leadership* may not exist, we do know that historically, leadership has always been defined on male, as opposed to female, terms. In American politics and in business and military circles, strong leadership is defined as an attempt to exert one's will over a particular situation, and this view has been indoctrinated into the consciousness of most Americans through the traditional interpretation of our national history. This view of leadership, in turn, affects how the public will view other aspiring leaders, particularly women.[7]

This conceptualization of leadership on male terms has often served as a barrier for women in politics, not only for those seeking elected office but for those holding political office as well. The policymaking process in the United States is viewed as the reallocation of resources within society, with the winners exerting their power and influence over the losers within the political arena. Because men are traditionally expected, due to stereotypes, to be competitive, strong, tough, decisive, and in control, the male view of leadership better fits the American political model. Women, on the other hand, are expected, again due to stereotypes, to exhibit traits that are cooperative, supportive, understanding, and show a willingness to serve others. Other female characteristics of leadership include using consensus decision making, viewing power as something to be shared, encouraging productive approaches to conflict, building supportive working environments, and promoting diversity in the workplace. Gender, socialization, and chosen career paths all play an important role in defining leadership and in explaining the differences in the leadership styles of women and men.[8]

Scholars interested in studying gendered differences in leadership show that in some areas, particularly politics and business, women often bring "a more open, democratic, and 'people-centered' approach to their leadership positions." However, a more inclusive and participatory approach to leadership is not exclusive to women, and since women have yet to reach parity with men in leadership positions, not enough evidence exists to categorize leadership styles based on gender alone.[9] Differences between male and female leadership styles are sometimes subtle and should not be overstated. It is also important to point out that a "generic woman" does not exist when attempting to determine such differences, since race, class, ethnicity, age, and sexual orientation perhaps play even more important roles when determining the context of one's actions or behaviors in the political arena.[10] Nonetheless, using other countries as an example, women national leaders have exhibited diverse leadership styles—some more traditionally "male," like former British Prime Minister Margaret Thatcher, and some more traditionally "female," like former Philippine President Corazon Aquino.[11]

Does gender matter in the area of policymaking? First, it is important to note that not only is the electoral process in the United States male dominated, but our political institutions are male dominated as well. Once elected, women politicians tend to bring different priorities into the policymaking arena than their male counterparts.

Women are also more likely to work across party lines to achieve their goals, as witnessed by the leadership style of female members of the U.S. Senate in recent years. Both Democratic and Republican women in the Senate have made their collective voices heard on bipartisan issues affecting women, such as the Homemaker Individual Retirement Account (cosponsored by Democrat Barbara Mikulski of Maryland and Republican Kay Bailey Hutchison of Texas, which allows homemakers to invest as much money in these tax-free retirement accounts as their working spouses) and a resolution in support of mammograms for women in their forties (cosponsored by Mikulski and Republican Olympia Snowe of Maine).[12]

However, not all women politicians automatically support women's issues, since party affiliation (Democrat or Republican) and political ideology (liberal, moderate, or conservative) is still the most important predictor for bill sponsorship or the actual vote on a particular bill. One study on the state legislatures in California and Arizona showed that there is little difference between the behaviors, particularly in regard to meeting the needs of constituents, between male and female members. While women legislators often take the lead on women's issues, both male and female legislators showed a willingness to engage in a cooperative, democratic, and open manner in developing legislation to meet the needs of constituents— behaviors traditionally defined as female leadership traits.[13] Other studies have shown that whereas men can easily adopt leadership strategies that are viewed as either male or female, and be praised for doing so, women are viewed more negatively if they adopt a more traditionally male leadership style (being more competitive, tough, or decisive).[14]

Women politicians must work hard to survive in the male-dominated world of American politics, particularly in the image-driven, media-saturated political culture that now exists. More than four decades ago, Richard Neustadt provided the seminal definition of political power in his study of leadership and the American presidency—political power is the ability to effectively bargain and persuade to achieve political objectives.[15] During the television age, that ability to bargain and persuade dictates that politicians must be effective communicators as well as savvy in their dealings with the news media. Therefore, while discussing women and leadership within the political arena, it is also important to consider differences in how women communicate, are viewed by the American public, and how the press portrays them.

Research by communication and linguistics scholars shows that men and women communicate differently. In general, men view communication as negotiations where they must maintain power, an "individual in a hierarchical social order in which he [is] either one-up or one-down." Women view communication as an opportunity for confirmation, support, and consensus, "an individual in a net-work of connections."[16] This difference can actually benefit women politicians who must appear on television, either during a campaign or while in office. As a medium, television demands intimacy and the ability to express the "private" self; this is obvious in the trend of per-sonalizing politics throughout the 1990s. Male politicians more often discuss goals, while women politicians more often reveal themselves through an intimate, conversational, and narrational style of speech. Women politicians tend to have a greater comfort level in expressing as opposed to camouflaging themselves publicly, which can be quite useful in developing their public image.[17]

Negative stereotyping of women politicians, however, can harm that public image. Whether it is positive or negative, stereotyping, which is a method used to quickly categorize information about someone, is a common everyday occurrence. Negative stereotyping about women as ineffective or weak leaders can harm their success as candidates or officeholders. For example, research in recent years has shown stereotypes to exist about both male and female political candidates. Women, who are considered more compassionate, are seen as more competent in the traditionally female policy areas of health care, the environment, education, poverty, and civil rights. Men, who are considered more aggressive, show stronger compe-tencies in the traditionally male policy areas of military and defense matters, foreign policy, and economic and trade issues.[18]

Women in politics, especially those who have succeeded, have also traditionally been viewed by the news media as an anomaly—a unique occurrence that deserves attention because it is outside the norm.[19] Trivialization of women in the news media has also contin-ued, through portrayals on television and in the movies that can lead to "symbolic annihilation" of women in general,[20] as well as the stereotyping that occurs in news coverage of women candi-dates and politicians.[21] In many campaigns, news media coverage has added to the negative stereotyping of women candidates, thus hurting their efforts to win an elected office since the news media pay more attention to style over substance when covering female candidates. Many voters may doubt the policy qualifications of women candidates when news coverage downplays issues and highlights personal traits; this can develop less favorable images of women candidates.[22]

PLAN OF THE BOOK

In examining women and their role within American politics, this text is different than most other women and politics texts in that it looks at the core theme of women and leadership within the political arena. The topics found in this book provide the essential themes for understanding women and politics from a traditional political science perspective, while also considering the issue of women's leadership and the challenges associated with the current political environment (the importance of image, media, and money) as more women get elected to office (Congress and state governors), appointed to high-ranking federal positions (the executive and judicial branches), and as the United States moves closer to electing the first woman president. We will also consider the impact of women at all levels of the governing process—as citizens, voters, candidates, and officeholders—and how, in turn, government policies impact women. For example, how has the government dealt with "women's issues" (traditionally defined as domestic issues such as welfare, health care, education, etc.) in recent years? Why are certain public policies so important to women, and what are the obstacles (if any) in making necessary changes? And, do women politicians bring different perspectives to the policymaking process?

Many students ask, why study women and politics, as well as a related question, what is the difference between women and politics and women's studies? Women's studies as an academic discipline grew out of the women's movement in the late 1960s, and began as informal groups of students and professors interested in studying gender and asking questions about how women (as opposed to the generic term *man*) fit into the political and social order. Since then, and throughout the 1970s and 1980s, the existence of women's and gender studies programs have increased dramatically at the college and university level, as has the number of women and politics courses being taught within political science departments across the country. The two areas are intricately linked, through the development of feminist theories, as well as the methodologies (how we study issues) and core themes of studying women as women (the gendered meanings of social institutions, experiences, events, and ideas). Women's studies courses and programs are interdisciplinary, which means that ideas and methodologies come from a variety of disciplines (like political science, history, economics, psychology, philosophy, or communication, to name a few) and are brought together in an attempt to better understand the experiences of women in many facets of life.[23]

The study of women and politics also grew out of the women's movement along with the development of women's studies courses and programs. Prior to the late 1960s, as the feminist movement grew within colleges and universities, only a handful of books or studies had ever been conducted about women as political actors. The study of women and politics grew rapidly throughout the 1970s and 1980s, as did the subfield of women and politics within the American Political Science Association. The study of women and politics is more specific than women's studies, focusing solely on women as political participants, officeholders, and policymakers, and how public policy at all levels of governing impacts women. All political scientists, not just those who call themselves women and politics scholars, have benefited from this expansion of disciplinary boundaries by raising questions about what political scientists study and how they study it. By considering "woman" as a category of study, "feminist political scientists have been able to call into question some of the central assumptions and frameworks of the discipline."[24] However, while the discipline of political science "now has gender on its agenda," much research remains to be done to better understand the role of race, class, party affiliation, and ideology in shaping how women politicians impact the policymaking process, as well as the role of the media in shaping perceptions of women leaders and how that may limit their political opportunities.[25]

This book is firmly grounded within the traditions of women and politics as it has evolved within political science, and it will also highlight the theme of political leadership throughout by providing examples and profiles of prominent women political leaders. Understanding the role that women play in American politics must begin with an examination of women as political participants. Chapter 2 will provide a historical analysis of the women's movement in America and its leaders, including the various phases of the women's movement and its generational differences (for example, the fight for suffrage culminating in 1920, followed by the drive for an equal rights amendment to the U.S. Constitution that began in 1923 and continuing until the amendment's close defeat in 1982). Understanding feminist theory is also relevant to studying women and politics, and this chapter will provide a brief discussion of feminist theory and its various classifications (liberal, radical, socialist, Marxist, black, Latina, etc.), and how feminism continues to influence women and politics today.

Next, how women participate in politics will be examined. Chapter 3 will take a look at women as voters and as members of political parties and interest groups. Important questions include: How do women vote and why, and is there truly a gender gap in American politics? Also, how do political parties and interest groups represent women's issues, and how do each court support from women? The socialization process, including the role of the news media, is also important to this discussion to determine how women think about politics in general, about their role as voters, and about policy issues relevant to them. Chapter 4 will look at women as political candidates, including the unique challenges that women have faced in running for office at all levels of government. Breaking into the system and becoming political leaders is not an easy task for women candidates, and we will consider the progress that women have made in state and national elections in recent decades. Also, what challenges do women face within the party structure and in raising adequate funds to finance campaigns? Is there gender bias in news media coverage during campaigns, and does this lead to negative stereotyping of women candidates?

The next three chapters will look at women as political leaders and officeholders. Chapter 5 will consider women within Congress and state legislatures, followed by women within the executive branch at the federal level and holding executive positions at the state and local levels in Chapter 6, and women within the federal and state judicial branches in Chapter 7. To what offices have women been elected or appointed, and have they made a difference in the areas of leadership, governance, and policymaking? Have women political leaders effectively raised public awareness of women's policy issues, or developed workable solutions? Do women governors or legislators govern differently than their male counterparts, or even differently from each other? What challenges do these women face in their careers, and how do those challenges differ from those faced by men? Chapter 6 will also ask a much talked about question in recent years: When will America elect its first woman president?

Finally, Chapter 8 will provide a concluding look at the progress that women have made in American politics, as well as address future challenges for women within the political process as voters, candidates, and political officeholders. Returning to the theme of leadership, we will consider how women impact the political and policymaking process as leaders and what trends may emerge in the future.

STUDY/DISCUSSION QUESTIONS

1. Why has leadership traditionally been defined on male, as opposed to female, terms? How has this served as a barrier to women's success in politics?
2. What role did the women's movement have on the academic study of women and gender, particularly within the field of political science?
3. How has the women and politics subfield within political science shaped our understanding of the category "woman"?

SUGGESTED READINGS

Burns, James MacGregor. 2003. *Transforming Leadership.* New York: Atlantic Monthly Press.

Freeman, Sue J. M., Susan C. Bourque, and Christine M. Shelton, eds. 2001. *Women on Power: Leadership Redefined*. Boston: Northeastern University Press.

Genovese, Michael A., ed. 1993. *Women as National Leaders*. Thousand Oaks, CA: Sage.

Jamieson, Kathleen Hall. 1995. *Beyond the Double Bind: Women and Leadership*. New York: Oxford University Press.

Northouse, Peter G. 2004. *Leadership: Theory and Practice,* 3rd ed. Thousand Oaks, CA: Sage.

Rhode, Deborah L., ed. 2003. *The Difference "Difference" Makes: Women and Leadership*. Stanford, CA: Stanford University Press.

Sapiro, Virginia. 2003. *Women in American Society: An Introduction to Women's Studies,* 5th ed. Boston: McGraw-Hill.

Tannen, Deborah. 1990. *You Just Don't Understand: Women and Men in Conversation.* New York: Ballantine Books.

ONLINE RESOURCES

http://cawp.rutgers.edu. Center for American Women and Politics, Eagleton Institute of Politics, Rutgers, State University of New Jersey.

http://www.apsanet.org/~wpol/. Home page for the Women and Politics Research Section of the American Political Science Association.

NOTES

1. Barbara Kellerman, "You've Come a Long Way, Baby—and You've Got Miles to Go," in *The Difference "Difference" Makes: Women and Leadership,* ed. Deborah L. Rhode, 54 (Stanford, CA: Stanford University Press, 2003).
2. Rhode, Introduction to *The Difference "Difference" Makes,* 6.
3. Susan C. Bourque, "Political Leadership for Women: Redefining Power and Reassessing the Political," in *Women on Power: Leadership Redefined,* ed. Sue J. M. Freeman, Susan C. Bourque, and Christine M. Shelton, 86–89 (Boston: Northeastern University Press, 2001).
4. See Peter G. Northouse, *Leadership: Theory and Practice,* 3rd ed. (Thousand Oaks, CA: Sage, 2004). Northouse outlines a variety of leadership theories, including approaches that focus on traits, skills, styles, situations, and personality.
5. James MacGregor Burns, *Leadership* (New York: Harper & Row, 1978).
6. James MacGregor Burns, *Transforming Leadership* (New York: Atlantic Monthly Press, 2003), 29.
7. M. Margaret Conway, Gertrude A. Steuernagel, and David W. Ahern, *Women and Political Participation: Cultural Change in the Political Arena* (Washington, DC: Congressional Quarterly Press, 2005), 112.
8. Northouse, 270–71.
9. Jean Stapleton, Introduction to *The American Women 2001–2002: Getting to the Top,* ed. Cynthia B. Costello and Anne J. Stone (New York: W.W. Norton, 2001), 33.
10. Rhode, *The Difference "Difference" Makes,* 5.
11. Michael A. Genovese, "Women as National Leaders: What Do We Know?" in *Women as National Leaders,* ed. Michael A. Genovese, 214–15 (Newbury Park, CA: Sage, 1993).
12. Catherine Whitney et al., *Nine and Counting: The Women of the Senate* (New York: William Morrow, 2000), 125–27.
13. Beth Reingold, *Representing Women: Sex, Gender, and Legislative Behavior in Arizona and California* (Chapel Hill: North Carolina University Press, 2000), 243.
14. Sue J. M. Freeman and Susan C. Bourque, "Leadership and Power: New Conceptions," in Freeman and Bourque, *Women on Power,* 8–9.
15. Richard Neustadt, *Presidential Power and the Modern Presidents: The Politics of Leadership From Roosevelt to Reagan* (New York: Free Press, 1990).

16. Deborah Tannen, *You Just Don't Understand: Women and Men in Conversation* (New York: Ballantine Books, 1990), 24–25.

17. Kathleen Hall Jamieson, *Beyond the Double Bind: Women and Leadership* (New York: Oxford University Press, 1995), 94–95.

18. Leonie Huddy and Nayda Terkildsen, "Gender Stereotypes and the Perception of Male and Female Candidates," *American Journal of Political Science* 37(1993):119–47.

19. Patricia Rice, "Women Out of the Myths and Into Focus," in *Women and the News* (New York: Hastings House, 1978), 45–49.

20. See Gaye Tuchman, *Hearth and Home: Images of Women in the News Media* (New York: Oxford University Press, 1978), 7–8; and David L. Paletz, *The Media in American Politics: Contents and Consequences,* 2nd ed. (New York: Longman, 2002), 135–39.

21. See Maria Braden, *Women Politicians and the Media* (Lexington: University of Kentucky Press, 1996).

22. Kim Fridkin Kahn, *The Political Consequences of Being a Woman* (New York: Columbia University Press, 1996), 134–36.

23. Virginia Sapiro, *Women in American Society: An Introduction to Women's Studies,* 5th ed. (Boston: McGraw-Hill, 2003), 7–10.

24. Susan J. Carroll and Linda M. G. Zerilli, "Feminist Challenges to Political Science," in *Political Science: The State of the Discipline II,* ed. Ada W. Finifter, 55–72 (Washington, DC: American Political Science Association, 1993).

25. Bourque, "Political Leadership for Women," 106.

The Women's Movement and Feminism in the United States

The true republic: men, their rights, and nothing more; women, their rights, and nothing less.

—*Motto of the weekly newspaper* Revolution, *edited by Susan B. Anthony*

*T*he women's movement in America, which entered its third century with the arrival of the new millennium in 2001, has had many highs and lows along the way. Whereas several political victories have been achieved, like gaining suffrage during the early part of the twentieth century, the women's movement has also experienced its share of setbacks, like the defeat of the Equal Rights Amendment (ERA) to the U.S. Constitution in 1982. It is especially important to note that not all American women have been a part of the women's movement or have agreed with the various policy changes that the movement has sought regarding a woman's public role. In general, the women's movement has sought the breakdown of what is known as the public versus private sphere, which had been the traditional way of life for men and women since the earliest days of the American colonies—the home was a woman's domain while public matters, including government and politics, were the sole responsibility of men. As a result, women had no public voice, and the laws that governed them in most cases did not view them as equal citizens in the eyes of the law.

From the start, those who affiliated themselves with the women's movement sought more equality and fairness for women, as well as an end to the patriarchal treatment of women in all aspects of their lives. Although there are many historical moments that have shaped the women's movement, as well as different policy outcomes that have been sought by the movement's various leaders, some common interests have survived the test of time. According to political scientist Anne N. Costain, "Throughout their long history, women's movements, whether labeled suffrage, temperance, women's liberation, or antislavery, are linked in their consistent cry for democratic inclusion—politically, economically, educationally, and in the professions."[1]

While this chapter is not meant to analyze every aspect of the history of the women's rights movement in America, it will highlight the broadly defined phases or "waves" of the women's movement as well as a few of the prominent women leaders that shaped the cause. The first wave is generally considered the fight for women's suffrage, beginning in 1848 at the Seneca Falls Convention and culminating with passage of the Nineteenth Amendment to the U.S. Constitution granting women the right to vote in 1920. The second wave of the women's movement emerged in the politically turbulent decade of the 1960s and coincided in part with the civil rights movement, with major attention focused on breaking down the legal barriers to sexual equality and, toward the end of this period, on the failed passage of the Equal Rights Amendment to the Constitution. However, this second wave is known for a narrow view of women's rights purported by mostly middle-to-upper-class white women. This period is followed by the third wave of the women's rights movement, which began in the 1990s and has focused on increased political participation by women as well as a more inclusive notion of women's rights to include racial, ethnic, and gender minorities. Later in the chapter, we will also consider the basic categories of feminist theory and how feminism continues to influence women as political leaders today.

THE FIRST WAVE OF THE WOMEN'S MOVEMENT IN AMERICA

Women have struggled with the issue of the public versus private sphere throughout our nation's history; that is, that men controlled the public sphere while women were relegated to the household and childrearing chores in the private or domestic sphere. Despite all the talk of liberty and that "all men were created equal" during the American revolutionary period, women in the American colonies were confined to domestic duties, and had few legal rights. Women during this period could not vote or hold public office, few had any kind of formal education, and divorce was difficult to obtain. In several colonies, married women could not own property and had no legal rights over their children.

However, "the revolutionary ferment offered women new opportunities and engendered in many a new outlook," as numerous women began to aid the war effort and help the American armies in their fight against the British by raising money, plowing fields, making ammunitions, and cooking, cleaning, and caring for the soldiers.[2] While most women remained in the private sphere during this era, a few outspoken women began to demand equal treatment during and after the war. As early as 1776, Abigail Adams, the future first lady and wife of John Adams, wrote to her husband with her now-famous demand for equality:

> "I long to hear that you have declared an independency—and by the way in the new Code of Laws which I suppose it will be necessary for you to make I desire you would Remember the Ladies, and be more generous and favourable to them than your ancestors. Do not put such unlimited power into the hands of the Husbands. Remember all Men would be tyrants if they could. If perticular care and attention is not paid to the Ladies we are determined to foment a Rebellion, and will not hold ourselves bound by any Laws in which we have no voice, or Representation."[3]

Unfortunately, John Adams and the other eventual framers of the constitution were not to be persuaded, and the legal status of women did not improve after the American Revolution or with the ratification of the U.S. Constitution in 1789 or the Bill of Rights in 1791. The rights of women were not addressed in the documents, and "by today's standards, it is impossible to deny that the original Constitution was a racist and sexist document or that the Framers wrote it in a way that benefited them."[4] As America moved into the nineteenth century, and as the nation began to experience rapid industrialization that moved the economy away from its agrarian roots, the "cult of domesticity" took a stronger cultural hold on women. The home became a safe haven from the cruel world outside, and it was the responsibility of women to civilize their husbands and children. It also became an accepted social norm that "men and women were designed by God and nature to inhabit 'separate spheres.'"[5] Legal and political rights for women remained much as they had been in the colonial era, with no right to vote, and little or no control over property or custody of children.

The formal women's rights movement began in 1848 at the Seneca Falls Convention, convened by Lucretia Mott and Elizabeth

Cady Stanton. Most women who attended had been active in the abolitionist movement for years, even decades. The idea for the convention had been born following the 1840 World Anti-Slavery Convention in London, where female delegates, including Mott and Stanton, had not been allowed to participate and were even forced to sit behind a partition so as not to be seen. Prior to the Seneca Falls Convention, Stanton wrote her famous "Declaration of Sentiments and Resolutions," a bold document declaring the rights of women modeled after the Declaration of Independence. Stanton's "Declaration" demanded economic and property rights, and denounced many things, including slavery, discrimination in education, exploitation of women in the workforce, the patriarchal family, and divorce and child custody laws. She also denounced organized religion as "perpetuating women's oppression."

Suffrage would become the major issue of the latter stages of the first wave of the women's movement, but that was not the initial case of the claims that came out of Seneca Falls:

> Popular belief has it that the nineteenth-century movement focused solely on suffrage, but that became true only in the movement's later, diluted form. At Seneca Falls, the demand for suffrage was almost an afterthought, a last-minute item Stanton tacked on to the list—the only resolution not unanimously supported. In fact, at its inception, this movement was radical and multi-issued. It named male power over women "absolute tyranny."[6]

Yet, securing the right to vote did emerge as the major issue for the movement, since women's activists like Stanton, Alice Paul, and Susan B. Anthony believed suffrage to be the most effective way to gain access to the political system and change the unjust way that women were viewed in the eyes of the law. They also eventually realized that slavery would end and that all men regardless of race, but not women, would be given the right to vote following the passage of the Thirteenth, Fourteenth, and Fifteenth Amendments to the Constitution (in 1865, 1868, and 1870, respectively). Thus, a nearly 75-year struggle ensued to earn the right for women to vote. Many of the leaders of the women's movement had gained leadership and organizational skills as activists in the abolitionist movement, so for many generations of suffragists, the strategy to achieve what at the time seemed like a radical change to the constitution included protests, marches, lectures, writings, and various forms of civil disobedience.

From the start, Stanton and Anthony remained prominent leaders within the suffrage movement. Both had been active in the American

Equal Rights Association (AERA), which had been formed in 1866 to fight for universal suffrage. However, the organization disbanded in 1869 due to internal conflicts involving the political priorities of the group (whether or not woman's suffrage should be a higher priority than black male suffrage). In May 1869, Stanton and Anthony formed the National Woman Suffrage Association (which would eventually become the League of Women Voters in the 1920s, and is still in existence today). Led by Anthony, the NWSA preferred fighting for a constitutional amendment to give women the right to vote nationally. A second group, the American Woman Suffrage Association (AWSA), was formed in November 1869 by Lucy Stone and Henry Blackwell to fight for suffrage on a state-by-state basis. Anthony had gained national attention for the cause of adding a constitutional amendment to give women the vote, as well as much needed support, when she was arrested and tried for voting in the 1872 presidential election. The amendment, first introduced in Congress in 1878, would be presented to 40 consecutive sessions of Congress until it finally passed as a proposed amendment in 1919.[7]

Along the way, the suffrage movement faced fierce opposition from a variety of antisuffrage groups. Big business (particularly the liquor industry), the Catholic Church, and political machine bosses feared that women voters would support political reform. Women led many of the temperance efforts of the late nineteenth and early twentieth centuries in an attempt to ban the sale of alcohol. Other organizations, like the National Consumer's League formed in 1899, and the National Women's Trade Union League formed in 1903, worked to change labor conditions for various corporations. Many southern states also opposed women's suffrage because they did not want African American women to gain access to voting rights, or argued that suffrage was a states-rights, not a federal, issue.[8] Just as they did in the suffrage movement, women emerged as strong leaders in the antisuffrage movement as well. The women leaders in both movements tended to be among the social elite—educated, with access to money and having important social contacts. But many women did not support the breakdown of the public versus private sphere dichotomy, fearing that women would lose their power and influence within the domestic sphere and among social networks if forced to become participants in public life. As a result, it is important to remember that women's suffrage, or later political efforts within the women's movement, did not universally represent all women, as we will discuss later in this chapter.

Between 1878 and August 1920, when the Nineteenth Amendment was ratified, activists for women's voting rights relied on a variety of strategies to gain support for the proposed amendment. Legal strategies were used in an attempt to invalidate male-only voting laws, while others sought to pass suffrage laws at the state level. Some women fighting for the cause could not be deterred, enduring hunger strikes, staging rallies or vote-ins, or even being jailed for publicly campaigning for the amendment. The movement became revitalized with an influx of younger women joining the fight in 1910 due to immigration, urbanization, and an expanding female labor force; the cause also won a state referendum in Washington granting women the right to vote that same year. California would follow in 1911, and by 1912, a total of nine western states had passed legislation giving women the right to vote. (As a territory, Wyoming had granted women full suffrage in 1869, and retained the law when it became a state in 1890. The other six western states included Colorado, Utah, Idaho, Arizona, Kansas, and Oregon.)

Another major turning point came in 1916 when a coalition of suffrage organizations, temperance groups, women's social welfare organizations, and reform-minded politicians pooled their efforts and resources to wage a fiercer public battle. The political tide began to turn in the suffragists' favor in 1917, when New York adopted women's suffrage legislation. Then, in 1918, President Woodrow Wilson also changed his position and backed the constitutional amendment. On May 21, 1919, the House of Representatives passed the proposed amendment, followed by the Senate two weeks later. Tennessee became the 36th state to ratify the amendment on August 18, 1920, which gave the amendment the necessary three-fourths support from the states (it was officially certified by Secretary of State Bainbridge Colby eight days later on August 26, 1920). Few of the early supporters for women's suffrage, including Anthony and Stanton, lived to see the final political victory in 1920.

In the immediate postsuffrage era, several women's rights activists, including Carrie Chapman Catt and Alice Paul, sought to capitalize on the momentum of finally receiving the vote and began to lobby Congress for an Equal Rights Amendment to the Constitution. Catt, a leader of the suffrage movement, had served as president of the National American Woman Suffrage Association (NAWSA), which was formed in 1890 when the NWSA and AWSA had merged, from 1900 to 1904, and again from 1915 until ratification of the nineteenth Amendment in 1920. Catt then founded the League of Women Voters that same year. Paul had been instrumental in pushing the suffrage cause to victory as head of the NAWSA's Congressional Committee, but left that organization in 1913 to form the Congressional Union for Woman Suffrage (which became the National Women's Party in 1917). In 1923, Paul drafted the Equal Rights Amendment and the National Women's Party presented it to Congress. Beginning that same year, Congress annually considered various versions of an ERA, yet never passed a constitutional amendment for the states to consider. To amend the U.S. Constitution, a two-thirds vote is necessary in both the House of Representatives and the Senate to propose the amendment for consideration by the states. For ratification, three-fourths of the states (38 of 50) must approve the amendment. Finally, in 1972, after intense lobbying by groups such as the National Organization for Women (NOW) and Business and Professional Women (BPW), Congress passed the proposed ERA. The contents of the proposed amendment were brief and to the point:

> Section 1. Equality of rights under the law shall not be denied or abridged by the United States or by any State on account of sex.
> Section 2. The Congress shall have the power to enforce, by appropriate legislation, the provisions of this article.
> Section 3. The Amendment shall take effect two years after the date of ratification.

By 1973, 22 states had ratified the amendment, but by the initial deadline of 1978, only 35 states had signed on for ratification. In spite of an extended deadline to 1982, momentum for passage faltered under intense opposition from religious groups such as the National Council of Catholic Women and the Mormon Church, as well as political groups opposed to the ERA such as the Eagle Forum led by Phyllis Schlafly. Many observers have noted that the ERA "divided rather than united women politically and culturally."[9] Not only were women divided over whether to support the amendment, various opinions existed as to whether the amendment would really make a difference in terms of legal rights for women. Some argued that the amendment was merely symbolic, while others feared that passage would do away with various legal protections for women in the workplace, as well as those involving child support and exemption from military registration.

After the initial excitement of the proposed constitutional amendment, public support and political enthusiasm waned in the years leading up to the deadline set for 1982. Although passage of the amendment would have been a political victory for the women's rights movement, many of the gender-based classifications that ERA supporters hoped to outlaw had already been changed through

FAILURE IS IMPOSSIBLE:

The Political Leadership of Elizabeth Cady Stanton and Susan B. Anthony

When discussing the early women's rights movement in America, perhaps no two women were as influential as Elizabeth Cady Stanton and Susan B. Anthony. Due to the lasting partnership that the two developed in pursuing women's rights and women's suffrage, one's contribution to the cause cannot be discussed without also considering the contributions of the other. Each had unique leadership strengths that seemed to perfectly complement the other: "Stanton was the leading voice and philosopher of the women's rights and suffrage movements while Anthony was the powerhouse who commandeered the legions of women who struggled to win the ballot for American women."[10] Stanton and Anthony also exemplify what political scientist Bruce Miroff calls "dissenting leadership," a model of leadership for a group that was "denied the fundamental rights of citizenship and was excluded from participation in public life."[11]

Stanton (1815–1902) is known as the "founding mother of feminism" and is remembered as the "boldest and most brilliant leader of the feminist movement in nineteenth-century America."[12] The wife of prominent abolitionist Henry Stanton and mother of seven, Stanton was 32 years old when she helped convene the Seneca Falls Convention in 1848. A graduate of Troy Female Seminary, she refused to be merely what she called a "household drudge," and when she and Henry married, the word *obey* was omitted from the ceremony. They honeymooned in London while attending the World Anti-Slavery Convention in 1840. After Stanton's call for a woman's right to vote at Seneca Falls, she was opposed by fellow organizer Lucretia Mott as well as her husband, both of whom thought the idea was too radical. Soon after, in 1850, Stanton met and developed a lifelong friendship and partnership with Susan B. Anthony, who joined in Stanton's cause for women's rights and women's suffrage. In 1866, Stanton ran for the House of Representatives, the first woman to ever do so, when she realized that while New York prohibited women from voting, the law did not prohibit them from running for or holding public office. Her election bid was unsuccessful.

Prior to her years as an activist force within the women's rights movement, Anthony (1820–1906) had become a teacher at the age of 17. After teaching for 15 years, she became active in the temperance movement, considered one of the first expressions of American feminism by dealing with the abuses of women and children who suffered from alcoholic husbands. As a woman, however, Anthony was not allowed to speak at public rallies. Consequently, she helped found the Woman's State Temperance Society of New York, one of the first women's associations of its kind. After meeting Stanton in 1850, she soon joined the women's rights movement and dedicated her life to achieving suffrage for women. Unlike Stanton, Anthony never married and did not have the burden of raising children. As a result, she focused her attention on organization within the movement, and was more often the one who traveled, lectured, and canvassed nationwide for suffrage. Anthony was arrested for attempting to vote on more than one occasion beginning in 1872, but remained committed to her endless campaign for a constitutional amendment allowing women the right to vote. In 1900, Anthony persuaded the University of Rochester to admit women, and she remained a lecturer and activist for the cause of suffrage until her death.

Together, Stanton and Anthony formed the Women's Loyal National League in 1863 in New York City to demand the end of slavery. In 1868, they founded the Workingwoman's Association that sought to improve working conditions for women, and also started a weekly newspaper aptly named the *Revolution*, which demanded, among other things, equal pay for women. The following year, they founded the National Woman Suffrage Association after they both sought a more radical solution than had been proposed by the American Equal Rights Association. Stanton served as president of the organization for 21 years, in spite of the fact that she differed with Anthony's view of the need for suffrage to be the single issue dominating the woman's rights movement. Stanton, "known for her searching intellect, wide-ranging views, and radical positions," is remembered as the "preeminent women's-rights theorist of nineteenth-century America."[13] Anthony, who became the first woman to have her image appear on any form of U.S. currency with the Susan B. Anthony dollar's debut in 1979, is remembered as the woman most identified with women's suffrage and passage of the Nineteenth Amendment.[14] Together, their early brand of political leadership shaped the lives of millions of American women.

Supreme Court rulings, legislation in Congress, or through presidential executive orders. According to political scientist Jane J. Mansbridge, the defeat of the amendment was not all that surprising: "[T]he puzzle is not why the ERA died but why it came so close to passing. . . . The irony in all this is that the ERA would have had much less substantive effect than either proponents or opponents claimed."[15] Yet, the ERA remained a prominent rallying call for the feminist leaders of the second wave of the women's movement.

THE SECOND WAVE: THE MODERN WOMEN'S MOVEMENT

While the fight for the ERA certainly played an important role in the modern women's movement, several other issues began to take center stage for American women throughout the 1960s as the movement entered its second wave. With similarities to the civil rights movement throughout the decade, the mainstream women's rights movement turned its attention to ending the cult of domesticity that had been the ideal during the 1950s. Women had made great progress during the 1940s in the workforce during World War II, when millions of American men served in the military leaving a variety of jobs open for women. However, many of those women who had experienced professional success and were seen as patriots by helping out the American economy during the war were displaced from their jobs when the soldiers returned home. The start of the postwar baby boom era in the late 1940s, coupled with the new trend of suburbanization across the nation, left the lives of most American women once again dominated by responsibilities in the private sphere.

The publication of Betty Friedan's book, *The Feminine Mystique*, became one of the most important events for the women's rights movement in the early 1960s. A 1942 graduate of Smith College, Friedan had spent 10 years as a suburban New York wife and mother doing occasional freelance writing when she circulated a questionnaire among her Smith classmates in 1957 to determine their satisfaction with their lives. When she discovered that they were resoundingly dissatisfied with their life experiences as wives and mothers, and with her undergraduate training in psychology, Friedan embarked on a much more intensive analysis that resulted in *The Feminine Mystique*'s publication in 1963. The book immediately struck a chord with millions of American women who shared

Friedan's view that many women were trapped in the supposed domestic bliss of hearth and home and that women had no real identity by simply living vicariously through their husbands and children. The book became an immediate, yet controversial, best seller. Known for discussing "the problem that has no name," Friedan showed that

> virtually every powerful cultural institution—magazines, television, advice books, schools, and religious leaders—prescribed a middle-class ideal for women: they were to be wives and mothers, nothing more, nothing less. . . . Suburbs gave a new, geographic twist to the old split between private and public, family and work, personal and political. The work suburban women actually did, inventing new forms of creative motherhood and elaborating networks of volunteer institutions, was not seen as, well, *real* work.[16]

The response that Friedan received from thousands of letters written by women from various social backgrounds, telling the author that the book had changed their lives, convinced her that a new chapter in the women's movement had been born. And although she had not originally sought such a position, Friedan became the leader of this new wave of the movement. Taking this new leadership role seriously, she began touring the country to talk about practical solutions to some of the problems that women, particularly in the workforce, were facing, such as a lack of affordable day care and flexible work schedules and maternity leaves to accommodate family needs. Inspired by the civil rights movement, Friedan declared the need for a "women's NAACP." In October 1966, she cofounded the National Organization for Women (NOW), a civil rights group dedicated to achieving equality for women in American society. As NOW's first president, serving in the post until 1970, Friedan lobbied for an end to gender-classified employment notices, for greater representation of women in political office, for child care centers for working mothers, and for legalized abortion and other political reforms. In 1969, she became a founding member of the National Abortion Rights Action League, and in 1971 she also became a founding member of the National Women's Political Caucus (as discussed in Chapter 5). Throughout the 1970s and early 1980s, Friedan also worked as an outspoken proponent for passage of the ERA.[17]

Membership in NOW and other women's organizations grew rapidly during the early 1970s as the women's rights movement capitalized on the political momentum first started a decade earlier. President John F. Kennedy had formed the Commission on the Status of

Women in 1961 in response to concerns about women's equality, and based on the commission's various studies at both the national and state levels that showed pay inequity based on sex, Congress passed the Equal Pay Act in 1963. Other political victories for sexual equality came within the decade with Congress' passage of Title IX of the Educational Amendments Act of 1972, which required equal opportunity for women in all aspects of education including admissions, financial aid, and funding for women's athletic programs. Congress had also finally passed the Equal Rights Amendment that same year. And in 1973, the Supreme Court, in *Roe v. Wade*, struck down state laws banning abortion in the first three months of pregnancy. Advocates for women's rights saw the decision as a major victory since reproductive rights and the ability of women to control their own bodies was on the forefront of their political agenda.

But not all American women were on board with this new wave of the women's rights movement, and not all believed in the causes supported by Friedan and other prominent feminists at that time such as Gloria Steinem (see below), Susan Brownmiller (an early organizer of this phase of the women's movement and best-selling feminist author), and Flo Kennedy (an attorney and civil rights–women's rights activist who was also the first black woman to graduate from Columbia Law School). Despite the changing workforce in America, where a two-income family became the norm throughout the 1970s and 1980s, many working women did not consider themselves feminists. The victory for pro-choice feminists in legalizing abortion also galvanized the pro-life movement at the national level, and those organizations opposed to passage of the ERA also gained national prominence. Under the leadership of Phyllis Schlafly, the Eagle Forum, founded in 1972, fought to stop passage of the ERA and to protect what their members believed to be traditional family values and the traditional role of women in society, which they believed was being harmed by feminists. Another group, Concerned Women for America (CWA), also became a prominent antifeminist and anti-ERA group. Founded in 1979 by Beverly LaHaye, the wife of fundamentalist Baptist minister and Moral Majority cofounder Tim LaHaye, the mission of CWA was to promote biblical values in all areas of public policy. Both organizations are still in existence. The formation of these groups in response to those supporting the women's rights agenda shows the diversity of viewpoints, even by the 1970s, about a woman's role in society. As historian Ruth Rosen points out, "Insecure in their separate worlds, women privately sniped at each other: housewives blasted activists as unpatriotic; working women derided housewives as spoiled and lazy; and housewives accused working women of neglecting their children."[18]

Divisions even emerged within the women's movement, as more moderate feminists (who tended to represent the view of middle-to-upper-class white women) clashed with more radical feminists (who wanted to broaden the movement beyond the pursuit of legal equality to bring about more radical change for women within all aspects of society). By the 1980s, the women's rights movement had succeeded with many legislative and legal changes in granting equality to women, even with the failure of the ERA. Yet the debate over the role of women in American society would continue into the 1990s and beyond as a younger generation of feminists weighed in with their views of where the women's rights movement had been and where it should go in the future.

THE THIRD WAVE:
GENERATION X AND BEYOND

By 1990, many political observers believed that feminism in America was dead. But according to women's studies scholar Astrid Henry, the publication of two key books in 1991—*Backlash: The Undeclared War on American Women* by Susan Faludi and *The Beauty Myth: How Images of Beauty Are Used Against Women* by Naomi Wolf—began to challenge the idea that the women's movement was over. Both Faludi and Wolf represented a "new generation of popular feminist writing" that helped reinvigorate interest in the women's movement.[19] Faludi wrote about how the gains, both political and legal, made by women during the 1970s had been followed by a backlash during the 1980s, a decade in which a conservative Republican—President Ronald Reagan—dominated the political environment. Wolf pointed out some of the key differences in the women's movement generations, since those who had fought the battles in the heyday of the second wave did not necessarily represent the same attitudes and beliefs of younger feminists. Other events during this time period also contributed to the renewed public interest in women's issues, including the Supreme Court confirmation hearing of Clarence Thomas in the fall of 1991, as well as the increased number of women running for public office in 1992 (as we

GLORIA STEINEM:

Feminist Leader and Cultural Icon

Known as a feminist leader, journalist, best-selling author, and social activist, Gloria Steinem has been one of the most enduring forces within the women's movement since the 1960s. Now in her early 70s, there are few areas of Steinem's life that have not become part of the public dialogue about feminism and the women's movement. Her celebrity status, and her desire to remain unconventional, has also kept her in the news for decades; from the early days of the modern women's movement, the fact that she was physically attractive seemed to defy the media's stereotype of what it meant to be a feminist. Early in her career as a freelance journalist, she infiltrated the Playboy Club as an undercover "bunny" to write an expose about how women employees were sexually harassed and discriminated against in the New York club. She went public with the fact that she had had an abortion during the 1950s while she was in college, a time when the procedure was still illegal in the United States. She had a four-year relationship with Mort Zuckerman, the Republican publisher of *U.S. News and World Report,* and once had to deny a relationship with former Secretary of State Henry Kissinger after they were photographed together in public. In 2000, she made headlines again when, at the age of 66, she married for the first time (an institution she had long railed against as destroying a woman's identity and as an "arrangement for one and a half people").

In terms of her political accomplishments, Steinem was among the leaders of the women's rights movement in the late 1960s and early 1970s in the campaign for reproductive rights, equal pay and equal representation, and an end to domestic violence. She helped found the National Women's Political Caucus in 1971, as well as the groundbreaking *Ms. Magazine* and the Ms. Foundation for Women in 1972. She is also a founding member of the Coalition of Labor Union Women, and her books *Outrageous Acts and Everyday Rebellions* (1983) and *Revolution from Within: A Book of Self-Esteem* (1992) are best-sellers. When *Ms. Magazine* first appeared as a one-time insert in *New York Magazine* in December 1971, no one gave a magazine dedicated to women's rights and feminist views a chance for survival against the traditional women's magazines that gave "advice about saving marriages, raising babies, or using the right cosmetics." But the 300,000 test copies sold out nationwide in only eight days, generating 26,000 subscription orders. According to the *Ms.* Web page, "few realized it would become the landmark institution in both women's rights and American journalism that it is today. . . . [It] was the first national magazine to make feminist voices audible, feminist journalism tenable, and a feminist worldview available to the public."[20] The magazine's success and ability to survive for three decades is even more impressive given the fact that it has remained free of advertising for most of its existence. Steinem has been involved with the magazine, either as an editor or writer, for all but a few years of its publication.

Steinem is also known for her compelling, and sometimes controversial, quotes about how women have been treated in American society. Among the most notable include her comments, "If the shoe doesn't fit, must we change the foot?" and "A woman without a man is like a fish without a bicycle" (the latter phrase was first coined by Australian author Irina Dunn, but often attributed to Steinem as well). Steinem continues to speak out about feminist issues and causes, and acknowledges the many changes the women's movement has undergone in the past four decades. While women of her generation rebelled against the pressures to marry, have children, take their husband's name, and be the picture of "femininity," Steinem now acknowledges that many women in the twenty-first century now embrace the traditional notion of being a wife and mother, but that women have the choice to lead their life devoted to family, a career, or both. In a January 2005 interview, she stated that although being a wife and mother are no longer "social imperatives" like they were several decades ago, the women's movement is no way diminished and is still necessary: "It's like saying, 'We're living in a post-democracy.' It's ridiculous. We've hardly begun. The good news is that American feminism used to be three crazy women in New York: now a third of the country self-identify as feminists, and 60% if you go by the dictionary definition."[21] Clearly, the debate over feminism and the women's movement lives on.

will discuss in Chapters 4 and 5). Images of strong women were also suddenly prominent in Hollywood, with the release of the movie *Thelma & Louise* in 1991 (about two women fighting back against male violence, which grossed more than $45 million) and the popularity of two top-rated sitcoms starring women—ABC's *Roseanne* (named for the star of the show, who portrayed a strong-willed mother in a working-class family in a small midwestern town) and CBS's *Murphy Brown* (starring Candice Bergen as a single and successful 40-something star political reporter of a television network news show set in Washington, DC).[22]

What is now referred to as the third wave of the women's movement got its start in the political and social environment of the early 1990s. Unlike the second wave of the women's movement, which largely focused on equality and the inclusion of women in traditionally male-dominated areas, the third wave (also known as postfeminism) continues to challenge and expand common definitions of gender and sexuality. The third wave, which represents those young feminists born between 1965 and 1974, also seeks to move beyond the political battles—equal access to work, education, and athletics—that the older generation of feminists had fought before them. This wave of the women's movement reflects the unique view of women's issues and feminism in the generation of women who came of age mostly in the 1980s, where feminism had already been part of the world in which they grew up. Third wave–Generation X feminists began moving beyond the monolithic, white, middle-class views of earlier feminism to embrace a more multicultural view that included women of all races, ethnicity, and socioeconomic backgrounds. Not only has a more global view of women's issues emerged, but a common theme is found in labeling the third wave a prowoman movement, as opposed to the stereotype of antiman that became part of the image of feminists during the late 1980s and early 1990s.[23] The difference between the two generations, according to Henry, remains a crucial part of the identity for third wave feminists: "This refused identification, or disidentification, is frequently with or against second-wave feminism. . . . [F]or many younger feminists, it is only by refusing to identify themselves with earlier versions of feminism—and frequently with older feminists—that they are able to create a feminism of their own."[24]

Today's younger feminists are also called "stealth feminists," due to the media's backlash of painting the women's movement as a negative association. Until the early 1990s the media kept talking about the end of feminism, yet younger generations of women began reshaping the movement with various articles and books about the third wave agenda.[25] According to Debra Michaels,

> beyond endless accounts of young women from so-called Generations X, Y, and Z renouncing feminism with the oft-repeated, "I'm not a feminist, *but. . .,*" lay another reality: countless thirty-something women not only embracing the label but defining our lives as torchbearers for feminism. In our careers, relationships, childraising strategies (or decisions *not* to have children)—in all our choices—"Stealth Feminists" have been quietly, invisibly, and sometimes even subconsciously continuing the work of the Women's Movement.[26]

Prominent third wave authors include Jennifer Baumgardner and Amy Richards, who point out that many women of their generation take women's rights and feminism for granted, which causes one of the biggest challenges for the movement: "[F]or anyone born after the early 1960s, the presence of feminism in our lives is taken for granted. For our generation, feminism is like fluoride. We scarcely notice that we have it—it's simply in the water."[27]

Politically, the third wave of the women's movement has also focused on candidate recruitment, campaign resources, democratic inclusion of women, more public roles for women, and finding a new voice for feminism through grassroots political activism. Their agenda has also included acknowledging the issues associated with economically disadvantaged as well as racial, ethnic, and gender minorities. There is a strong link to the Democratic Party, particularly during President Bill Clinton's administration as "softer" women's issues came to the forefront during the economic prosperity of the 1990s, including education, family, jobs, and health care. At the start of the 1990s, national security took a back seat in the national debate with the end of the Cold War. Following the terrorist attacks on September 11, 2001, the national debate would again change with national security issues eclipsing domestic issues. This, along with a trend supporting conservative Republican victories in Congress (since 1994) and the White House (since 2000), has made the pursuit of the third wave agenda on the national level more challenging for today's feminist leaders.[28]

FEMINISMS AND AMERICAN POLITICS

There is no simple or single definition for the word *feminism*. First used by American women fighting for suffrage at the turn of the twentieth century, the term was more broadly used by the women's movement in the 1970s in an attempt to bridge the many ideological and policy issues that divided women activists at the time. According to historian Sara M. Evans, the deep differences among feminists cause some to "regularly challenge others' credentials as feminists. . . . yet the energy of the storm that drives them all comes from their shared challenge to deeply rooted inequalities based on gender."[29] To borrow a broad definition of feminism from political scientist Barbara Arneil, it is the

> recognition that, virtually across time and place, men and women are unequal in the power they have, either in society or over their own lives, and the corollary belief that men and women should be equal; the belief that knowledge has been written about, by and for men and the corollary belief that all schools of knowledge must be re-examined and understood to reveal the extent to which they ignore or distort gender.[30]

Despite the problems associated with categorizing various modes of feminist thought, the "old labels" are still useful as they "signal to the broader public that feminism is not a monolithic ideology, that all feminists do not think alike, and that, like all other time-honored modes of thinking, feminist thought has a past as well as a present and a future."[31] While the following discussion does not include every category of feminist thought, the most prominent feminist categories are highlighted. It should be noted that many feminist "theories" have been developed and promoted by academic scholars, and there is sometimes a disconnect between the ideas promoted in these theories and their practical applications by political leaders within the women's rights or feminist movement.

Liberal feminism is grounded in the quest for equal rights and fairness in society for women (for example, in access to educational and employment opportunities, equal pay, and equal treatment in the eyes of the law). The first and second waves of the women's movement were greatly influenced by classical liberal thought, based on the writings of John Locke and John Stuart Mill among others, which emphasizes the value of individual rights, limited government, government by consent, competition, rational thought, and a government system based on the right over the good (meaning that procedural justice and fairness is more important than substantive justice). As a result, liberal feminism is based on the belief that "female subordination is rooted in a set of customary and legal constraints blocking women's entrance to and success in the so-called public world."[32]

Moving beyond the liberal tradition, **radical feminism** seeks to change the political and legal roots of patriarchy to also include a radical overhaul of social and cultural institutions (like the family and the church). Radical feminists believe that sexism must be eradicated, and that sex-gender roles that cause women's oppression within society must be changed. Various subgroups of radical feminists exist, but the two main groups include radical-libertarian and radical-cultural feminists. Radical-libertarian feminists believe that "the very concept of femininity as well as women's reproductive and sexual roles and responsibilities often serve to limit women's development as full human persons."[33] Radical-cultural feminists believe that the differences between men and women serve as barriers that "empower men and disempower women," yet they argue that being feminine is better than being masculine. Therefore, women should not try to be more like men since there are fundamental personality differences between men and women, and that women's differences are special and should be celebrated.[34] In general, radical feminists support the notion that there are biological differences between men and women and attempt to draw lines between biologically determined behavior and culturally determined behavior in order to free both men and women as much as possible from their previous narrow gender roles within society.

Another long-standing view of feminist thought includes **Marxist-socialist feminism.** Relying on the basic premise of socialist beliefs found in the nineteenth-century writings of Karl Marx, this group of feminists believes that capitalism and patriarchy work together to oppress women within society. As a result, political, social, and economic structures need reform and wealth must be redistributed to promote equality. There is a gendered division of labor within society, and women's work is always undervalued or devalued. Under the Marxist view of capitalism, those controlling the means of production control workers; the few control the many through private business ownership. To break the cycle of a society based on economic classes, a socialist system (meaning government control and ownership) must be created so that the means of production are owned by all within society and not just a powerful few. Marxist-socialist feminists believe that this type of reform will give women greater power and equality within the public sphere.

In response to the narrow and exclusive view of feminism during the second wave of the women's rights movement, women of color began to promote a more humanist view of feminism based on the intersection of race, class, and gender. As a result, **black feminism, Chicana feminism,** and **Latina feminism** emerged and brought a unique contribution to feminist thought, since these women have experienced two forms of discrimination within society based on their gender and racial or ethnic background. Their respective views provide a better balance to the feminist theories supported by educated white women. The black feminist movement grew out of, and in response to, the black liberation movement and the women's movement during the 1960s as many black women felt they were being racially oppressed in the white-dominated women's movement and sexually oppressed by the male leadership in the black liberation movement. Black feminists wanted to develop a theory that would adequately address the way race, gender, and class were interconnected and to take action to stop racist, sexist, and classist discrimination.[35]

Similarly, the Chicana feminist movement also emerged during the 1960s as Chicana feminists assessed both their life circumstances and their participation in the larger Chicano social protest movement. The policy concerns considered most pressing for Chicanas included welfare rights, reproductive rights, health care, poverty, immigration, and education.[36] The political mobilization of Latina feminists has also been shaped by similar concerns about employment, poverty, education, health, child care, and reproductive rights, as well as political empowerment within their communities. The term *Latina* is often broadly used to include different ethnic backgrounds, including Mexican American, Cuban American, Puerto Rican American, Central American, and Latin American. Most recently, however, the ethnic term *Latina/Latino* is used inclusively to refer to any person of Latin American ancestry residing in the United States (and also connotes identification with Indo-American heritage rather than Spanish European heritage). Latina feminists share a strong allegiance with other feminists of color in the United States.

Various other views of feminist thought have emerged within academic and political circles in the years since the second wave of the women's movement. **Postmodern feminists** reject classical liberal labels and believe that social, cultural, and political categories are socially constructed. As such, postmodern feminists want to deconstruct the notion of "truth" as we know it and offer a critique of liberalism and the systems and categories that privilege men over women. This view presents both a dichotomy and dilemma for feminists, since the postmodern view suggests that there is no inherent legitimacy to the current system. While feminists have succeeded by labeling women as privileged groups (through legislation and court cases), postmodern feminists claim that labeling women as a separate group within society is a worthless exercise.

The views of **multicultural** or **global feminists** suggest that all women are not the same and that cultural, racial, and ethnic differences among women should be acknowledged; one class of privileged, mostly white, women cannot speak for all women on the issue of equality and rights. **Psychoanalytic feminism** deals with the way society constructs masculine and feminine behavior, and argues that femininity is rooted in social expectations from early childhood behaviors separating males from females, thus taking root in women's psyches. As a result, a more humanist or androgynous approach is necessary to move away from the emphasis on male and female traits. **Gender feminism** is similar in that there is a psychological explanation, as well as a biological one, that explains the differences between masculine and feminine traits. Finally, **ecofeminism** argues that women and nature are connected and are both harmed by patriarchy's hierarchical system of oppression. This theory rests on the basic principle that patriarchal philosophies are harmful to women, children, and other living things. Parallels are drawn between society's treatment of the environment, animals, or resources and its treatment of women.

CONCLUSION

The story of the women's movement, women's rights, and feminisms in the United States is a diverse and complex history of how women have banded together and also clashed with each other in an attempt to define their preferred place in American society. The public versus private sphere that served to define a woman's role has long been the catalyst for numerous generations of women fighting for political and legal equality. No one movement, cause, or theory can encapsulate the needs of all women, yet significant progress has been made since the nineteenth century in bringing about political and legal reforms in regard to women's equality. Prominent women leaders such as Elizabeth Cady Stanton, Susan B. Anthony, Carrie Chapman Catt, Betty Friedan, Gloria Steinem, and countless others dedicated much of their lives to fighting for the right for women to enter the public realm at various points in our nation's history. While many barriers for women entering public life have been torn down, many challenges still lie ahead for women political leaders today. As we will discuss in the following chapters, women in today's political environment still face many obstacles in terms of entering the political arena, yet the legacy of the modern women's movement has provided many more opportunities for women in the public sphere than any prior generation.

STUDY/DISCUSSION QUESTIONS

1. Why was the first wave of the women's movement so closely tied to both the temperance and abolitionist movements during the nineteenth century?
2. Discuss the impact that Elizabeth Cady Stanton's and Susan B. Anthony's leadership had on the early women's rights movement.
3. Why did it take nearly 75 years after the Seneca Falls Convention for women to earn the right to vote in the United States?
4. What is meant by the public–private sphere split, and why did feminists view this as oppressive to women?
5. What influence did Betty Friedan's *The Feminine Mystique* have on the second wave of the women's movement?
6. How does the third wave differ from the second wave of the women's movement?
7. How do liberal and radical feminists differ? What impact have women of color had on feminist views and debates?

SUGGESTED READINGS

Arneil, Barbara. 1999. *Politics & Feminism.* Oxford: Blackwell.

Baumgardner, Jennifer, and Amy Richards. 2000. *Manifesta: Young Women, Feminism, and the Future.* New York: Farrar, Straus and Giroux.

Collins, Patricia Hill. 1990. *Black Feminist Thought: Knowledge, Consciousness, and the Politics of Empowerment.* Boston: Unwin Hyman.

Evans, Sara M. 2003. *Tidal Wave: How Women Changed America at Century's End.* New York: Free Press.

Friedan, Betty. 2001. *The Feminine Mystique* (with an Introduction by Anna Quindlen). New York: W.W. Norton.

Henry, Astrid. 2004. *Not My Mother's Sister.* Bloomington: Indiana University Press.

Jeydel, Alana S. 2004. *Political Women: The Women's Movement, Political Institutions, the Battle for Women's Suffrage and the ERA.* New York: Routledge.

Kolmar, Wendy K., and Frances, Bartkowski. 2005. *Feminist Theory: A Reader,* 2nd ed. New York: McGraw-Hill.

Mansbridge, Jane J. 1986. *Why We Lost the ERA.* Chicago: University of Chicago Press.

Matthews, Jean V. 1997. *Women's Struggle for Equality: The First Phase 1828–1876.* Chicago: Ivan R. Dee.

Morgan, Robin, ed. 2003. *Sisterhood Is Forever: The Women's Anthology for a New Millennium.* New York: Washington Square Press.

Rosen, Ruth. 2000. *The World Split Open: How the Modern Women's Movement Changed America.* New York: Penguin Books.

Tong, Rosemarie Putnam. 1998. *Feminist Thought: A More Comprehensive Introduction,* 2nd ed. Boulder, CO: Westview Press.

ONLINE RESOURCES

http://www.nwhp.org. The National Women's History Project.

http://www.cr.nps.gov/nr/travel/pwwmh/index.htm. Places Where Women Made History.

http://www.susanbanthonyhouse.org. The Susan B. Anthony House.

http://www.feminist.org. Feminist Majority Foundation.

http://www.thirdwavefoundation.org. The Third Wave Foundation.

http://www.now.org. National Organization for Women.

http://www.msmagazine.com. *Ms. Magazine.*

http://www.eagleforum.org. The Eagle Forum.

NOTES

1. Anne N. Costain, "Paving the Way: The Work of the Women's Movement," in *Anticipating Madam President,* ed. Robert P. Watson and Ann Gordon (Boulder, CO: Lynne Rienner, 2003), 31.

2. George Brown Tindall and David E. Shi, *America: A Narrative History,* 4th ed. (New York: W.W. Norton, 1996), 273.

3. Quoted in Phyllis Lee Levin, *Abigail Adams: A Biography* (New York: St. Martin's Press, 1987).

4. Lee Epstein and Thomas G. Walker, *Constitutional Law for a Changing America: A Short Course,* 2nd ed. (Washington, DC: Congressional Quarterly Press, 2000), 6–7.

5. Jean V. Matthews, *Women's Struggle for Equality: The First Phase 1828–1876* (Chicago: Ivan R. Dee: 1997), 5.

6. Robin Morgan, Introduction to *Sisterhood Is Forever: The Women's Anthology for a New Millennium*, ed. Robin Morgan (New York: Washington Square Press, 2003), xxxiii–xxxiv.

7. For example, see Alana S. Jeydel, *Political Women: The Women's Movement, Political Institutions, the Battle for Women's Suffrage and the ERA* (New York: Routledge, 2004), 46–48.

8. Ibid., 80.

9. David M. O'Brien, *Constitutional Law and Politics*, Vol 2, *Civil Rights and Civil Liberties*, 5th ed. (New York: W.W. Norton, 2003), 1479.

10. Judith E. Harper, "Biography of Susan B. Anthony and Elizabeth Cady Stanton," *PBS*, accessed at http://www.pbs.org/ stantonanthony/resources/index.html.

11. Bruce Miroff, *Icons of Democracy: American Leaders as Heroes, Aristocrats, Dissenters, & Democrats* (Lawrence: University Press of Kansas, 2000), 125.

12. Ibid., 125–26.

13. Lois W. Banner, "Elizabeth Cady Stanton," in *The Oxford Companion to United States History*, ed. Paul S. Boyer, 742 (New York: Oxford University Press, 2001).

14. Ellen C. DuBois, "Susan B. Anthony," in Boyer, *The Oxford Companion to United States History*, 38–39.

15. See Jane J. Mansbridge, *Why We Lost the ERA* (Chicago: University of Chicago Press, 1986), 1–7.

16. Sara M. Evans, *Tidal Wave: How Women Changed America at Century's End* (New York: Free Press, 2003), 18–19.

17. See Betty Friedan, *It Changed My Life: Writings on the Women's Movement* (New York: Random House, 1978).

18. Ruth Rosen, *The World Split Open: How the Modern Women's Movement Changed America* (New York: Penguin Books, 2000), 35.

19. Astrid Henry, *Not My Mother's Sister* (Bloomington: Indiana University Press, 2004), 16–17.

20. "HerStory," *Ms. Magazine*, accessed at http://www.msmagazine. com/about.asp.

21. Melissa Denes, *The Guardian*, "Feminism? It's Hardly Begun," January 17, 2005, accessed at http://www.guardian.co.uk/g2/ story/0,3604,1391841,00.html.

22. Ibid.

23. See Evans, *Tidal Wave*, 230–32.

24. Henry, *Not My Mother's Sister*, 7.

25. For example, see Barbara Findlen, ed., *Listen Up: Voices from the Next Feminist Generation* (Seattle: Seal Press, 1995); and Rebecca

Walker, ed., *To Be Real: Telling the Truth and Changing the Face of Feminism* (New York: Anchor Books, 1995).

26. Debra Michaels, "Stealth Feminists: The Thirtysomething Revolution," in Morgan, *Sisterhood Is Forever,* 139.

27. Jennifer Baumgardner and Amy Richards, *Manifesta: Young Women, Feminism, and the Future* (New York: Farrar, Straus and Giroux, 2000), 17.

28. Costain, "Paving the Way," 36.

29. Evans, *Tidal Wave,* 2–3.

30. Barbara Arneil, *Politics & Feminism* (Oxford: Blackwell, 1999), 3–4.

31. Rosemarie Putnam Tong, *Feminist Thought: A More Comprehensive Introduction,* 2nd ed. (Boulder, CO: Westview Press, 1998), 1.

32. Ibid., 2.

33. Ibid., 47.

34. Ibid., 47–49.

35. See Patricia Hill Collins, *Black Feminist Thought: Knowledge, Consciousness, and the Politics of Empowerment* (Boston: Unwin Hyman, 1990), 221–38.

36. See Alma M. García, "The Development of Chicana Feminist Discourse, 1980," *Gender & Society* 3, no. 2 (1989): 217–38.

CHAPTER 3

Women as Political Participants

I am a governor who happens to be a woman.

—Former New Jersey Governor Christine Todd Whitman
in response to a reporter's question on what it was like to be a woman governor

*I*n the last few presidential elections, the most sought after votes for both Democratic and Republican candidates have been those of women voters. Whether courting "soccer moms" (considered mostly college-educated, upper-middle-class, suburban, and predominantly white women with school-age children) in 1996, or "security moms" (women whose concerns about terrorism and national security now compete with more traditional women's issues such as education and health care) in 2004, presidential contenders and their strategic advisors have targeted women as the key to winning a presidential election. In 2004 in particular, undecided women voters were targeted in swing states by the campaigns of both incumbent Republican George W. Bush and Democrat John Kerry, if for no other reason than voter turnout among women has been higher than for men in each presidential election since 1980. That same year, what is now commonly referred to as the gender gap (which is the difference in the proportion of women and men voting for a particular candidate) became evident. Since that time, Democrats have maintained an advantage with women voters, and Republicans have continued in their efforts to close the gap. In 2004, significant efforts were made to increase the number of women who register and vote by both parties, especially among the large number of undecided women voters late in the presidential contest. And while women voters preferred Kerry to Bush by a margin of 7 percent, Bush still won the popular vote with 51 percent overall.[1]

Regardless of gender, voter turnout in general remains an issue in the United States, as we rank lower than many other industrialized democracies in this regard (including Belgium, Italy, France, Denmark, Austria, Germany, Great Britain, Canada, and Japan). The U.S. government is based on democratic principles with a strong emphasis on citizen participation. This distinguishes a democratic society from other types of government where citizens are not involved in the election of officials or the policymaking process. For the United States, it means that sovereignty lies with the people; for self-government to work, people have a right and an obligation to participate in government. But people must be given meaningful opportunities to participate, and the level of that participation is a measure of how fully democratic the society is. Women did not have the right to participate in the political process as voters until 1920 with the passage of the Nineteenth Amendment, but even then, not all women rushed to the ballot box to cast their vote in elections, and public opinion at the time still did not favor women's full participation in public life. Due to factors such as social, cultural, and legal barriers, women throughout our nation's history have never been encouraged to become full political participants. Even by the start of the twenty-first century, women were still contending with negative stereotypes that served as barriers to increasing their level of political participation. This chapter will consider women as political participants—as voters, as members of political parties and interest groups, and as members of the news media. It is important to learn how women vote and why, and to consider the significance of the gender gap in American politics. Also, how do political parties and interest groups represent women's issues, and how do each court support from women? The socialization process, including the role of the news media, is also important to this discussion to determine how women think about politics in general, about their role as voters, about policy issues relevant to them, and how they view women candidates as potential political leaders.

WOMEN AND POLITICAL SOCIALIZATION

How women define themselves as political participants occurs through the process of political socialization, which is how people acquire their political opinions, beliefs, and values. There are several agents of socialization, and many of them overlap. Early in one's life, these agents include family members and school. Parents can be very influential on a child's early beliefs, and many adults end up having the same political party affiliation and views on certain policies as their parents. What children learn in school, especially at the primary level, has been shown to teach children an idealized and heroic version of American history and politics. Studies have also shown that college-educated adults tend to show stronger support for individual rights and political involvement and awareness. Peer groups can also influence how one thinks about political issues, since these groups tend to have similar political views and being a member of the group can reinforce what a person already believes. Religion and attending church are also important agents of political socialization, as are political leaders and political institutions. One of the more powerful influences on the political socialization process is the mass media, which can provide strong images and can greatly influence stereotypical views of women in society. Even more directly related to the political process is the impact of the news media, which can affect one's political views by framing news in a certain way or through the process of agenda setting (deciding which stories are covered versus which ones are not). The news media may not be able to tell people what to think, but they can tell us what to think about.

As we discussed in Chapter 2, the split between the public and private spheres has served as a formidable barrier for women wanting to enter politics in the United States, which has so often influenced negative attitudes about women's political participation. From the time women first received the right to vote in 1920, that negative cultural attitude about women's political participation has represented an informal barrier to those seeking public office. As the century wore on, public opinion polls showed a slow decrease in the percentage of Americans who believed that women did not belong as participants of the political process or as officeholders. Cultural attitudes began to change more rapidly by the start of the modern women's movement in the 1960s, as women also began having more success in political campaigns. Yet, the political socialization process continues to plague women's efforts in the political arena as girls traditionally have not been socialized to take an active role in politics, with several studies showing that girls tend to show less interest in and have less knowledge of politics than boys. However, women most likely to run for office and be politically active had parents who voted in every election and encouraged their daughters to run for office while growing up.[2]

Political attitudes toward women in politics have changed as more women have been elected to office, moving away from the outdated belief that women did not belong in public life. According to political scientist Kathleen A. Dolan,

> A public that believes that a woman's place is in the home is unlikely to vote for any woman candidates with the courage to run. However, if voters feel that women have an equal role to play in political life, they can use these attitudes as a baseline against which they can evaluate individual women candidates and decide if they are worthy of support. . . . [T]he increased success of women candidates during the past 30 years or so has been mirrored by a gradual shifting in attitudes about women's place in political life.[3]

In terms of political attitudes, how women view other women as potential candidates may also be driven by traditional social norms about "appropriate" female behavior. According to political scientist Ruth B. Mandel, woman may face a cultural barrier to winning elected office due to the

> incongruence between their sex-role socialization and the characteristics and behavior necessary to wage a successful campaign. Although socialized to exhibit values and behaviors considered appropriate for females, in running for office women enter into a sphere of life dominated by masculine values and behavior patterns.[4]

As more women win campaigns and hold political office, the view of women as political leaders will more than likely continue to shift public attitudes about the efficacy of women in public life.

WOMEN AND THE MASS MEDIA

As one of the most important agents of political socialization, the mass media, and more specifically the news media, play an important role in how women are viewed as current or potential political leaders. Theories abound among scholars about how people receive information through the mass media. Some scholars suggest that the media have a powerful impact on society and that people may actually need to be protected from its effects. For example, viewers can be led to believe that reality mirrors the images in the mass media and that women and minorities can develop poor self-esteem due to negative stereotyping by media sources. A contrasting theory, known as the minimal effects approach, suggests that the mass media are weak in the impact on society, since people only expose themselves to media content that goes along with their current views or perceptions. Other theories, like the uses and gratifications approach or the media systems dependency approach, suggest that people have a strong purpose in their use of media to be informed, entertained, or to escape from their daily routines (with some people even becoming dependent on this use).[5]

What image is being portrayed about women through the mass media? Throughout the 1970s, movies and television were male dominated. Women were relegated to traditional and stereotypical roles: wife, mother, and homemaker, or for those women not married, looking for love, romance, and marriage. Women were not portrayed as independent or career oriented and were willing to give up their identities and ambitions for their husbands. Political news about women was mostly nonexistent and left to the women's pages of newspapers, including coverage of the women's movement and the founding of the National Organization for Women in 1966. Even into the 1980s, according to political scientist David L. Paletz, the mass media took a rather narrow view of its portrayal of women:

> Television's ideal feminine type was blonde, beautiful, and young; lesbians and African-American women did not fit. Aging in women was depicted more negatively than in men, and older women were hard to find in television shows, other than on *Golden Girls*, where they behaved as if they were much younger.[6]

The current representation of women is mixed—part traditional, part feminist. While some portrayals of women in films and on television starting in the 1990s finally began to reflect the diversity of women in American society in terms of race, ethnicity, socioeconomic status, education, occupation, marital status, and sexual preference, Paletz states that "ambivalent and contradictory images" of women remain as "women are told to assert themselves, pursue careers, enjoy their independence; but also to defer to men and to work hard to look beautiful and thin. The media's overtly political content continues to represent and reinforce the 'political dominance of males over females.'"[7]

The mass media also perpetrate many negative stereotypes about women in American society. Stereotyping is the act of using a simplified mental image of an individual or group of people who share certain characteristics or qualities; this allows people to quickly process information and categorize people based on what are often negative characteristics. In the political arena, voters also rely on sex stereotyping when forming impressions of political candidates, including some negative stereotypes about women candidates' leadership ability or qualifications for office. In certain situations, stereotyping of women candidates can be helpful. For example, if a particular elected position (like a mayor or state legislator) requires a great deal of effort in dealing with policies related to children or elderly people, then stereotyping a woman candidate as being caring and compassionate could actually be seen as beneficial. Yet, that same stereotype of a woman being more caring and compassionate than a male counterpart can be seen as a negative quality for a woman running for the White House, since a president is expected to lead with tough and bold initiatives in the area of defense and foreign policy.[8]

News coverage of women in general, but particularly of professionals and athletes, often relies on stereotyping, and women are drastically underrepresented in news coverage across all news outlets. Even with the steady increase of women in all professions—including politics, law, medicine, higher education, and the corporate world—most news coverage continues to rely on men, and not women, as experts in their respective fields. Women in the news are more likely to be featured in stories about accidents, natural disasters, or domestic violence than in stories about their professional abilities or expertise. This lack of gender balance in news coverage is an international problem, as a study by the Association for Women Journalists found in 2000. The organization studied news coverage of women and women's issues in 70 countries, and found that only 18 percent of stories quote women, and that the number of women-related stories came to just over 10 percent of total news coverage.[9] A lack of news coverage for women politicians can be particularly problematic if they are not portrayed as strong and capable leaders and as authoritative decision makers when it comes to public policy. This can be a difficult cycle to break because women in Congress, for example, do not receive as much attention due to lack of seniority and leadership positions. [10] Yet breaking the negative stereotypes of women and the portrayal of women as the political "other" in the news media is necessary to help facilitate the continued progress of women in government.

An important factor to also consider is the number of women working in the news media industry, as well as the number of women in high-ranking positions within the industry. Even with the progress that women in general have made in a variety of professions in the past four decades, still only one-third of all journalists in the United States are women, with the highest percentages at weekly newspapers and news magazines and the lowest at wire services and in television.[11] Women in journalism had made great strides by the early 1990s, holding more positions within the industry than ever before, but still held very few positions at the highest levels of decision making within the news media industry. Women journalists have, in recent years, begun to broaden the definition of news to include more policy issues relevant to women, including women's health, child care, economic issues, and issues dealing with sexual discrimination and sexual harassment.[12] Yet the news media is still dominated by white men, both within news organizations and in the coverage that is produced. Therefore, the social and cultural norms that are reflected in a majority of news coverage do not represent the views of women or ethnic minorities, since "these internal constraints of media organizations and personnel, by necessity, dictate the ultimate news product."[13]

On the other hand, media outlets dedicated to women (as opposed to the mainstream news industry) have moved way beyond the women's pages of newspapers from the 1960s and 1970s to become a multibillion-dollar industry, run in part by many powerful and influential women known as the "spin sisters." Women's magazines alone, like *Glamour*, *Cosmopolitan*, *Woman's Day*, *Good Housekeeping*, *Redbook*, and *Ladies' Home Journal*, just to name a few, are part of a $7 billion-a-year industry. Network television targets much of its news programming in the morning (like NBC's *The Today Show* and ABC's *Good Morning America*) and in primetime (NBC's *Dateline*, ABC's *Primetime* and *20/20*, and CBS's *48 Hours*) at women viewers, with an emphasis on emotional human-interest stories or the latest consumer news about health risks. Cable television has also discovered the power of women as a demographic group with advertisers (women are considered much more influential in purchasing decisions than men) with networks such as Lifetime (whose motto is "television for women") and Oxygen (whose stated mission is to bring women "the edgiest, most innovative entertainment on television"). The afternoon talk-show circuit is still dominated by Oprah Winfrey, one of the wealthiest and most powerful women in America, along with other successful talk shows in the past decade with hosts such as Rosie O'Donnell and Ellen DeGeneres. While this part of the media industry may be run by the spin sisters, the message to women readers and viewers may not always be positive. According to Myrna Blyth, a former spin sister and editor of a major women's magazine, the message in women's media is not only negative and often misleading but also comes with a liberal bias:

I know from long experience that media for women tells you end-lessly about the stress in your life, about the way you should look, about what should make you feel sorry for yourself, or very, very fearful about your health and the environment. In much the same way you are given a one-sided message about politics, too, by al-ways being told more government is the best solution to fix many of the problems in your life. That's a philosophically loaded mes-sage that is the culmination of all the other stories you are told about how tough life is for women, even middle-class women.[14]

WOMEN AS VOTERS

Between 1920, when women first gained the right to vote, and 1980, women voted at lower rates than men. There are several explanations for this trend, including a backlash from the antisuffrage movement in the early part of the century with many women still not wanting to vote, to a lack of positive political socialization for young girls and women encouraging them to become active political participants well into the 1980s. However, that trend has reversed itself during the last three decades. Since 1980, and in every subsequent presidential elec-tion, women have voted at a higher rate than men. For example, roughly 7.8 million more women than men voted in 2000, which helps explain the attention that political parties and presidential candidates have paid to the "women's vote" in recent campaigns. In 2004, a non-partisan effort called "Women's Voices, Women's Vote" targeted un-married women, along with respective partisan efforts by the Bush (W Stands for Women) and Kerry (Women for Kerry) campaigns.[15] While the most prominent issues during the campaign centered on terror-ism, national security, and the war in Iraq, subtler messages were be-ing promoted by both candidates to target women voters, particularly those women who were presumably undecided until the last few days of the campaign. Media strategies even included several appearances by both candidates and their surrogates (their spouses, children, re-spective running mates and *their* spouses and children) on popular daytime television shows with traditionally high female viewership like *The View*, *Live With Regis and Kelly*, and *Dr. Phil*. (George W. and Laura Bush and John and Teresa Heinz Kerry each made appearances on the latter show to talk about their respective marriages.)[16]

Since 1980, much scholarly and news media attention has been paid to this issue of a gender gap in American elections, which explains the differences between men and women in their party

KATHERINE GRAHAM:
The Power Behind the Front Page

Both Katherine Graham (1917–2001) and her newspaper, *The Washington Post*, left an indelible mark on politics and the news media industry in America. Graham's father Eugene Meyer had purchased the *Post* in 1933 and served as its publisher until his death in 1946. Graham's husband Philip Graham then took over as publisher and was responsible for purchasing and including *Newsweek* magazine as part of the Washington Post Company. Philip Graham committed suicide in 1963, leaving his wife Katherine, a homemaker and mother of four, with control of the company. From 1969 until 1979 she served as publisher of the newspaper, and served as board chair and chief executive office of the company from 1973 until 1991, remaining chair of the executive committee until her death.

Due to the influence of the *Post*, not only within Washington but also throughout the nation and world as one of the leading news sources among political elites, Graham was considered one of the most powerful women in America.[17] Under her leadership as publisher, the *Post*, through the investigative work of reporters Carl Bernstein and Bob Woodward, led the news industry with its coverage to expose the Watergate scandal and played a prominent role in the resignation of President Richard Nixon in 1974 (the stories won the Pulitzer Prize for reporting). In 1971, she also allowed the *Post* (at the same time as *The New York Times*) to print excerpts from the top-secret Pentagon

identification and voting choice. In general, election results suggest that women are more likely to identify with and vote for the Democratic Party and its candidates while men are more likely to support the Republican Party and its candidates. Between 1980 and 1992, that gap between how men and women vote for president had remained between a 4 to 8 percent difference, raising to 11 percent in both the 1996 and 2000 presidential campaigns. Election results have shown that the gender gap is larger among white than non-white voters. It is also larger among voters at higher socioeconomic levels, among voters with more formal education, among unmarried voters, and among voters without children.[18] By the 2004

Papers, which detailed the history and decision-making process of American military involvement in Vietnam. This was done against the advice of the newspaper's attorneys and against government directives. In the famous *Pentagon Papers* case that came before the U.S. Supreme Court in the summer of 1971, the Nixon administration attempted, but failed, to stop the publication of the documents in both the *Post* and the *Times* by citing concerns for national security. A majority of the justices disagreed, and claimed that the federal government could not impose prior restraint on the nation's leading newspapers to stop publication of the stories. During this time period, the *Post* developed its strong reputation within the news industry for its hard-hitting investigations and solidified its position as a leader among nationally read newspapers.

In 1997 Graham published her memoirs, titled *Personal History*. The autobiography won the Pulitzer Prize in 1998, and was praised for its honest portrayal of her husband's mental illness (he suffered from manic depression) that led to his suicide. She was also honest about her trepidation in taking over the newspaper after her husband's death. As she stated, "I had very little idea of what I was supposed to be doing, so I set out to learn. What I essentially did was to put one foot in front of the other, shut my eyes, and step off the edge."[19] As a tribute, Graham's Washington funeral was broadcast live on major media outlets across the country, and brought together political and media elites to extol "her character, skill, and contributions" to the worlds of both journalism and politics.[20]

presidential election, the gender gap had been reduced to only a seven-point difference, with 48 percent of women versus 55 percent of men voting to reelect George W. Bush.

While the gender gap has narrowed, it has been replaced by an even larger marriage gap. Polling throughout the fall 2004 campaign showed that although Kerry had a narrower lead among women voters than past Democratic candidates have enjoyed, his lead among single voters, particularly women, was anywhere between 20 to 30 percent. On the other hand, Bush had nearly as wide of a lead among married voters, particularly women. The marriage gap has never been this wide, but pollsters suggested that it was attributed to fundamentally different views of government and the direction of the country. Married people are more optimistic about the future and are more suspicious about government's ability to help them [which favors] Republicans. Unmarried people tend to view government as more able to provide solutions to problems and are more pessimistic about the future of the country [which favors] Democrats.[21]

The first use of the term *gender gap* is credited to Eleanor Smeal, who talked about the trend while president of the National Organization for Women in 1981. American journalists quickly picked up on the phrase and popularized it as "convenient shorthand" to refer to gender differences in support for Democrats and Republicans. According to political scientist Pippa Norris, the role of gender in American politics helped create an electoral realignment in 1980, revealing a "seismic shift in voting choice and party identification, which has subsequently been consolidated over successive elections. This development has had important consequences for party competition, for the recruitment of women candidates for elected office, and for the salience of gendered issues on the American policy agenda."[22] However, Norris warns that the many aspects of the gender gap phenomenon require further study to better understand the complexities involved with gender and its impact on voting behavior:

> Gender realignment has now become an established part of American elections, taken for granted by commentators, journalists, and politicians. It provides a useful frame or "peg" on which to hang different stories about the election. Nevertheless, we should not be seduced by the conventional wisdom as many assumptions surrounding this phenomenon remain underexplained.[23]

One of the most important issues to point out about the gender gap is that it does not necessarily provide an advantage to one particular party (usually assumed to be the Democratic Party) or a particular candidate. It simply means that men and women vote differently.[24] It is also important to remember that women do not constitute a "monolithic voting bloc." As Richard A. Seltzer et al. point out in their study of women candidates, women as voters represent a "diverse and heterogeneous group of voters, not the special interest group that the term *the women's vote* implies. There are conservative and liberal women, anti-choice and pro-choice, women who oppose affirmative action and those who support it. The answer to the question 'What do women want?' depends on which women you ask."[25] Women candidates also do not automatically attract or win the support of women voters. While women do tend to support women candidates by a slight advantage in most elections, partisanship among voters is still a better predictor of the outcome of a race as opposed to the gender of the voter when a woman candidate is on the ballot. The gender gap can also vary across states, and can vary depending on the key issues being discussed by the candidates (the gender gap can widen when the media and candidates focus heavily on gender issues).[26]

WOMEN IN POLITICAL PARTIES AND INTEREST GROUPS

Although political parties and interest groups are not mentioned anywhere in the U.S. Constitution, they nonetheless play a crucial role in both the electoral and governing process in our nation at both the federal and state levels. Among other framers, James Madison in *Federalist 10* warned against the dangers of factions (what we would now consider a party or interest group) due to the potential for like-minded individuals to overtake the government based on popular passions for a particular issue. In spite of those warnings, and for better or worse, political parties developed and became a permanent part of our government in how we select officeholders and in how certain aspects of government, like Congress, are structured. Our Constitution also encourages and maintains a two-party system through its use of single-member districts (which is a winner-take-all system) where third-party candidates have little or no chance of gaining elected office. Interest groups also emerged throughout the nineteenth and twentieth centuries as an important way for the many diverse constituencies among the American electorate to band together and lobby government officials to either redress grievances or seek favorable policies and resources to benefit their particular policy agenda. Whereas women have never formed a like-minded or monolithic group in terms of the fight for equal rights or other relevant policy issues, "many, if not most, of the efforts through which women have sought power in American history have involved organized, collective action."[27]

Women as political activists within the American political system is not a recent phenomenon, nor is it something that occurred only once women secured the right to vote in 1920. Whether it was playing a crucial role in the suffrage movement, the abolition or temperance movements, or as political party volunteers or activists, women have participated in the political process on many levels since the mid-nineteenth century. Because political parties play such a large role in our electoral and governing process, it is important to understand how women have fit into the overall party structure. By the start of the twentieth century, the three types of female political activists included feminists, reformers, and party women. Feminists included those women working solely for suffrage, reformers represented a variety of interests, and party women belonged in both camps. According to Jo Freeman, who has written extensively on the history of women within political parties, after 1920, feminists and reformers struggled to survive while party women

> undertook the task of mobilizing women to vote. It was party women who had the resources, and the reason, to do this. And it was the ranks of party women who were augmented by the increased political interest in politics by women who had not been involved in anything political prior to 1920. . . . [T]he political parties recruited, organized, absorbed, and co-opted large numbers of politically inclined women.[28]

From 1920 throughout the mid-1960s, women's roles within political parties consisted of some work on party committees and through the creation of separate political clubs for women. Women did much work with few rewards, often with the public image of "worker bees" within the party, but still lacked much influence on policy issues. However, with the onset of the second wave of the women's movement during the late 1960s, this type of work within the parties laid the essential groundwork for women to play a larger role during the last three decades in terms of party platforms and policy agendas. As Freeman concludes, the presence of women in political parties throughout the twentieth century not only helped civilize politics by changing the male-dominated backroom approach to making decisions more accessible to women, but also "accelerated the shift in campaign techniques from emotional appeals to an emphasis on facts."[29]

In addition to how women have changed the internal structure within parties, the parties themselves have played a large role in shaping policy debates in an attempt to court women voters. It is therefore important to understand how political parties have responded to the changes in voters' attitudes about women's ever-expanding public role in recent decades, as well as to understand how Democrats and Republicans have differed on various women's issues. While the Democratic Party is associated most with the issues at the forefront during the second wave of the women's movement (most prominently support for the ERA, reproductive and abortion rights, and other legal issues such as pay equity and sexual harassment) and has continued to support feminist issues to the present day, it is actually the Republican Party that has a longer history of support for the ERA and other women's issues during the earlier decades of the twentieth century. The Republican Party platform consistently included the ERA from 1940 until it was dropped in 1980 with the party's nomination of Ronald Reagan (due to the conservative shift within the National Republican Party since then, the ERA has not returned to the platform). In contrast, Democrats were slow to publicly embrace or support the ERA. It did not receive consistent support in the party's platform, nor did all Democratic presidents embrace the idea. For example, although Democrat John F. Kennedy took several steps to address the issues presented to him from the President's Commission on the Status of Women, a committee that he established in 1961, he and his administration did not publicly support the ERA. On the other hand, Republican Richard Nixon, whose years in the White House (1969–1974) corresponded with rapid growth in the women's movement across the nation, went on record as a presidential candidate in 1968 in support of the ERA. The next two presidents, Republican Gerald Ford (1974–1977) and Democrat Jimmy Carter (1977–1981), would also publicly support and campaign for passage of the ERA.[30]

Since the 1980 election and the emergence of the gender gap, there are differences between the two parties in how they represent women's issues, although those differences are often not as stark as most would assume. As political scientist Kira Sanbonmatsu points out, the single issue of abortion is often mistakenly used as the standard-bearer of how parties differ on women's issues. Sanbonmatsu argues that Democrats and Republicans have presented a more moderate stance on women's issues, other than abortion, in recent years. Both parties continue to address women's issues, such as equality, workforce participation, and child rearing and family responsibilities, yet both parties "combine a mix of traditional and nontraditional views about the role of women." Democrats may be more attentive to women's issues than Republicans, yet "party leaders do not usually want elections to turn on gender debates."[31] Public opinion has also remained "ambivalent about the changing role of women" despite the often intense and heated rhetoric on gender-related issues among both interest group and party elites.[32] Aside from abortion, party platforms rarely offer conflicting policy stances on women's issues. In recent presidential elections, both parties have agreed on the importance of issues like enforcement of sex discrimination laws, better child care options, more funding for women's health issues, and strengthening the traditional family; however, there is "little discussion of women in

KIM GANDY:

Leading NOW into the Twenty-first Century

Since its founding in 1966, the National Organization for Women has witnessed many changes on the American political landscape. And while the women's movement and feminism has experienced many public highs and lows since the 1960s, NOW remains the largest feminist organization in the United States with more than 500,000 members and 550 chapters nationwide. The organization also counts among its former presidents feminist icons Betty Freidan, Eleanor Smeal, Molly Yard, and Patricia Ireland. The current president, Kim Gandy, has served in that role since 2001, taking over the top post following Ireland's 10-year tenure. Gandy, an attorney and former assistant district attorney in New Orleans, is a long-time activist who has served in leadership positions for NOW at the local, state, and national levels since 1973, including three years as Louisiana NOW president. In 1991, she directed the WomenElect 2000 Project, a nine-month grassroots organizing and recruiting effort in Louisiana that tripled the number of women in the state legislature and increased voter turnout among women to elect the first woman lieutenant governor in Louisiana.[33]

As the current president of NOW, Gandy faces the challenge of leading her organization during a time when the Republican Party, in control of both the White House and Congress, is pursuing a social conservative agenda that goes against almost every political issue that NOW supports. In addition to the traditional policy issues on NOW's agenda, like reproductive rights and equality for women in the workplace, Gandy has led the effort to publicly fight a variety of issues that the Bush administration has pursued, including the privatization of Social Security, Medicare reform, and a constitutional amendment banning same-sex marriages. In addition, NOW has pursued an aggressive strategy in its attempt to block the nomination of various conservative federal judges by the Bush administration.

politics, but the platforms are similar to the extent they discuss them."[34] The party leadership is also still male dominated, since there may be "parity in party organizational membership, [yet] party leadership for women remains rare."[35]

Although Gandy and NOW/PAC (a political action committee that supports feminist/women's rights candidates) endorsed Democrat John Kerry for president in 2004, he was not the organization's first choice. In August 2003, NOW/PAC, along with the National Women's Political Caucus, endorsed the candidacy of former U.S. senator and ambassador Carol Moseley Braun for the Democratic presidential nomination. According to a NOW press release, to receive such an endorsement, a candidate "must demonstrate an uncompromising commitment to the entire range of women's rights issues. . . . After considering the positions and past records of all the candidates lined up to challenge George W. Bush, one candidate stood above the rest. . . . Moseley Braun's candidacy is a prime example of what feminists strive for—women moving up through all levels of political office. We are proud to have this strong and accomplished woman running for the highest office in the land—and serving as an inspiration to women and girls of all ages who believe that a woman truly can become President of the United States."[36] The endorsement by the two women's groups, however, was called "silly" and Moseley Braun's campaign was called nothing more than a "vanity affair" by an editorial in *The New York Times*.[37] Taking issue with the opinion of one of the nation's most influential newspapers, Gandy responded: "One of the reasons women had to struggle so long to win the vote—and why we continue to fight for full equality—is the trivializing of women and our concerns. It smacks of sexism when the endorsement of two major women's organizations is demeaned as 'silly.' And it smacks of more than that when a qualified African-American woman is disparaged not for her experience or platform but for her presumed 'vanity.' . . . Moseley Braun, a forceful ally with a strong record, is getting women's issues onto the table and into the political debate—and she deserves our support. We've never made endorsements to impress the media or the pundits, and we're not going to start now. That would be silly."[38]

As we have already discussed, women have long been participants of activist causes and social movements. Women's interest groups have served as the vehicles for various causes of concern to women, and just as they did during the nineteenth century, continue to provide women with leadership experience and opportunities within the political arena. Through lobbying and public education efforts, women's interest groups now represent a wide array of issues and ideological stances and, through their political action committees (PACs) that provide monetary support for candidates, can play an influential role in election outcomes. Unlike political parties, which must represent numerous issues and constituencies under a wide umbrella, interest groups can focus on a much narrower range of policies and streamline their political or legislative efforts.

Older and more traditional women's interest groups include the League of Women Voters (LWV), the American Association of University Women (AAUW), and Business and Professional Women (BPW). The LWV, founded in 1920 by suffragist leader Carrie Chapman Catt, is a nonpartisan group dedicated to public education about political issues and candidates, and whose members educate citizens about and lobby for government and social reform legislation. Throughout its history, the LWV has been "an activist, grassroots organization whose leaders believed that citizens should play a critical role in advocacy." Both campaign finance and election reform have been recent policy priorities of the organization.[39] The AAUW, founded in 1881, promotes education and equity for women and girls, and its foundation also funds research on educational equity for girls and provides a legal advocacy fund for women who have experienced sexual discrimination in higher education. Similarly, BPW was founded in 1919 and promotes equity for women in the workplace through advocacy and education, including professional development programs, networking, and scholarship funds.

Newer women's interest groups emerged more as a result of protest politics during the second wave of the women's movement. Most prominent is the National Organization for Women, founded in 1966; the Women's Equity Action League, founded in 1968 (but disbanded in 1989); and the National Women's Political Caucus, founded in 1971. These organizations remain committed to pursuing a feminist agenda within American politics, including issues of equity, reproductive rights, and a variety of other public policies related to health care, welfare, child care, and the environment, just to name a few. Other groups also emerged as an alternative for women who do not support the feminist agenda, such as the Eagle Forum (founded in 1972), Concerned Women for America (founded in 1979), and the Independent Women's Forum (founded in 1992).

Women's PACs, which are founded by women to raise money primarily or exclusively for female candidates, have experienced tremendous growth in the past three decades. They have also made important financial contributions to women candidates in addition to providing training, consultation, and workers in support of their campaigns. These fundraising groups, "like female activists and candidates, ... extend across the partisan and ideological spectrum."[40] Four of the most prominent women's PACs include EMILY's List (which stands for Early Money Is Like Yeast, meaning "it makes the dough rise" in providing early seed money for campaigns) supports pro-choice Democratic female candidates; the WISH List (which stands for Women in the Senate and House), which supports pro-choice Republican female candidates; the Women's Campaign Fund, a nonpartisan group that supports pro-choice female candidates; and the Susan B. Anthony List, which supports pro-life female candidates (and claims that the group's namesake was opposed to legalized abortion). Women's PACs and their success are both "a product of and reaction to" the second wave of the women's rights movement. The current diversity among these groups is attributed, in part, to the polarization on gender-related issues and reproductive rights among the Democratic and Republican parties. Yet, as "divided as they are on fundamental questions about the role of government, [women's PACs] collectively have enhanced the representation of women in elective office. . . . [and] have altered the government agenda."[41]

CONCLUSION

As this chapter demonstrates, women have experienced a varied and diverse history in regard to their roles as participants in the American political process. While scholars continue to debate the significance of a gender gap in voting patterns, women continue to vote at a higher rate than men and still make up more than half of the voting population. Therefore, whether liberal or conservative, Democrat or Republican, or somewhere in between, women voters play a significant role in the development of campaign strategies and policy agendas at all levels of government. Women still have a long way to go to achieve more leadership positions within political parties, therefore reaching out to women voters across the ideological spectrum remains a top priority for both Democratic and Republican candidates. Gender issues have become part of the political branding process, since "at the end of the twentieth century the gender gap in party identification was no longer just a by-product of differences in ideology and socioeconomic status between men and women. Each party seems to have developed a gender-specific appeal based on its image and policies."[42] To date, no major realignment has occurred based on women's issues and those interest groups supportive of gender-specific issues do not dominate each party's agenda. However, increasing women's political participation in terms of voting, party and interest group leadership, as well as breaking down the negative stereotypes of women in the mass media and particularly those of women candidates in the news media, will go a long way to promoting women as political leaders at all levels of government.

STUDY/DISCUSSION QUESTIONS

1. How does political socialization impact political participation for women as voters and potential candidates? What are the contributing agents to political socialization?
2. What are some of the negative stereotypes of women portrayed in the mass media? How can stereotypes in news coverage of campaigns harm women candidates?
3. What is the gender gap among voters? How have voting patterns for men and women changed in recent decades?
4. How did women first enter party politics, and how do Democrats and Republicans differ in their support of women's issues?
5. What role do women's interest groups and PACs play in electing women of both political parties to public office?

SUGGESTED READINGS

Blyth, Myrna. 2004. *Spin Sisters: How the Women of the Media Sell Unhappiness—and Liberalism—to the Women of America.* New York: St. Martin's Press.

Braden, Maria. 1996. *Women Politicians and the Media.* Lexington: University Press of Kentucky.

Day, Christine L., and Charles D. Hadley. 2005. *Women's PACs: Abortion and Elections.* Upper Saddle River, NJ: Pearson/Prentice Hall.

Dolan, Kathleen A. 2004. *Voting for Women: How the Public Evaluates Women Candidates.* Boulder, CO: Westview Press.

Freeman, Jo. 2000. *A Room at a Time: How Women Entered Party Politics.* Lanham, MD: Rowman & Littlefield.

Norris, Pippa, ed. 1997. *Women, Media, and Politics.* New York: Oxford University Press.

Sanbonmatsu, Kira. 2002. *Democrats/Republicans and the Politics of Women's Place.* Ann Arbor: University of Michigan Press.

ONLINE RESOURCES

http://www.democrats.org/index2.html. The Democratic National Committee.

http://www.rnc.org. The Republican National Committee.

http://www.now.org. The National Organization for Women.

http://www.aauw.org. The American Association of University Women.

http://www.lwv.org. The League of Women Voters.

http://www.nwpc.org/index.htm. National Women's Political Caucus.

http://www.bpwusa.org. Business and Professional Women.

http://www.iwf.org. Independent Women's Forum.

http://www.emilyslist.org. EMILY's List.

http://www.thewishlist.org. The WISH List.

http://www.wcfonline.org. Women's Campaign Fund.

http://www.sba-list.org. The Susan B. Anthony List.

http://www.wvwv.org. Women's Voices. Women Vote.

NOTES

1. See "Gender Gap Persists in the 2004 Election," Center for American Women and Politics, Eagleton Institute of Politics, Rutgers, State University of New Jersey, November 5, 2004; and Susan Carroll, "Women Voters and the Gender Gap," American Political Science Association, accessed at http://www.apsanet. org/print/printer_content_5270.cfm.
2. See Nancy E. McGlen, Karen O'Connor, Laura van Assendelft, and Wendy Gunther-Canada, *Women, Politics, and American Society*, 3rd ed. (New York: Longman, 2002), 67–72.
3. Kathleen A. Dolan, *Voting for Women: How the Public Evaluates Women Candidates* (Boulder, CO: Westview Press, 2004), 42–43.
4. Ruth B. Mandel "A Question About Women and the Leadership Option," in *The Difference "Difference" Makes: Women and Leadership*,

ed. Deborah L. Rhode, 93–94 (Stanford, CA: Stanford University Press, 2003).

5. David L. Paletz, *The Media in American Politics: Contents and Consequences*, 2nd ed. (New York: Longman, 2002), 117–21.

6. Ibid., 135–37.

7. Ibid., 139.

8. See Kim Fridkin Kahn, *The Political Consequences of Being a Woman* (New York: Columbia University Press, 1996).

9. "Media Portrayals of Girls and Women," Media Awareness Network, accessed at http://www.media-awareness.ca/english/issues/stereotyping/women_and_girls/index.cfm.

10. Maria Braden, *Women Politicians and the Media* (Lexington: University Press of Kentucky, 1996), 18.

11. Doris A. Graber, *Mass Media & American Politics*, 6th ed. (Washington, DC: Congressional Quarterly Press, 2002), 94.

12. See David Weaver, "Women as Journalists," and Kay Mills, "What Difference Do Women Journalists Make?" in *Women, Media, and Politics*, ed. Pippa Norris (New York: Oxford University Press, 1997).

13. Lois Duke Whitaker, "Women and Sex Stereotypes: Cultural Reflections in the Mass Media," in *Women in Politics: Outsiders or Insiders?* 3rd ed. (Upper Saddle River, NJ: Prentice Hall, 1999), 95.

14. Myrna Blyth, *Spin Sisters: How the Women of the Media Sell Unhappiness—and Liberalism—to the Women of America* (New York: St. Martin's Press, 2004), 8.

15. Susan Carroll, "Women Voters and the Gender Gap," American Political Science Association, accessed at http://www. apsanet. org/print/printer_content_5270.cfm.

16. Lynn Sweet, "Courting the Ladies," *Chicago Sun-Times,* October 13, 2004.

17. Thomas R. Dye, *Who's Running America? The Bush Restoration,* 7th ed. (Upper Saddle River, NJ: Prentice Hall, 2002), 104.

18. Stephen J. Wayne, *The Road to the White House 2004: The Politics of Presidential Elections* (Belmont, CA: Thomson Wadsworth, 2004), 87.

19. Katherine Graham, *Personal History* (New York: Knopf, 1997).

20. Virginia Sapiro, *Women in American Society: An Introduction to Women's Studies* (New York: McGraw-Hill, 2003), 250.

21. Chuck Raasch, "Candidates Face Distinct Challenges in Courting Female Voters," *USA Today,* September 24, 2004.

22. Pippa Norris, "The Gender Gap: Old Challenges, New Approaches," in *Women and American Politics: New Questions,*

New Directions, ed. Susan J. Carroll, 146–47 (New York: Oxford University Press, 2003).

23. Ibid., 166.
24. Richard A. Seltzer, Jody Newman, and Melissa Voorhees Leighton, *Sex as a Political Variable: Women as Candidates & Voters in U.S. Elections* (Boulder, CO: Lynne Rienner, 1997), 4.
25. Ibid., 6.
26. Elizabeth Adell Cook, "Voter Reaction to Women Candidates," in *Women and Elective Office: Past, Present, & Future,* ed. Sue Thomas and Clyde Wilcox, 69–71 (New York: Oxford University Press, 1998).
27. Denise L. Baer, "Women, Women's Organizations, and Political Parties," in Carroll, *Women and American Politics,* 111.
28. Jo Freeman, *A Room at a Time: How Women Entered Party Politics* (Lanham, MD: Rowman & Littlefield, 2000), 4–5.
29. Ibid., 228–35.
30. See Janet M. Martin, *The Presidency and Women: Promise, Performance and Illusion* (College Station: Texas A&M University Press, 2003).
31. Kira Sanbonmatsu, *Democrats/Republicans and the Politics of Women's Place* (Ann Arbor: University of Michigan Press, 2002), 2.
32. Ibid., 91.
33. "NOW Officers, Kim Gandy—President," accessed at http://www.now.org/officers/kg.html.
34. Ibid., 112.
35. Baer, "Women, Women's Organizations," 134.
36. "NOW/PAC Endorses Carol Moseley Braun for President, Statement of NOW/PAC Chair Kim Gandy," August 26, 2003, accessed at http://www.now.org/press/08–03/08–26.html.
37. "NOW's Woman Problem," *The New York Times,* September 14, 2003.
38. "The *New York Times'* Woman Problem," Letter to the Editor by Kim Gandy, September 14, 2003, accessed at http://www.nowpacs.org/2004/letter.html.
39. See the League of Women Voters home page at http://www.lwv.org.
40. Christine L. Day and Charles D. Hadley, *Women's PACs: Abortion and Elections* (Upper Saddle River, NJ: Pearson/Prentice Hall, 2005), 1.
41. Ibid., 95.
42. Alan Abramowitz, *Voice of the People: Elections and Voting in the United States* (New York: McGraw-Hill, 2004), 99.

CHAPTER 4

Women as Political Candidates

A new political consciousness was born that no longer asked "why" a woman candidate, but "why not?" The real test of my candidacy will come when the next woman runs for national office.

—Geraldine Ferraro
on her vice presidential candidacy in 1984

If women make up slightly more than half of the population in the United States, which translates into more than half of eligible voters, then why are women still so underrepresented in elected political office? Since finally gaining the right to vote in 1920, women have been making up for lost time in many areas of the political process. Yet despite the gains made in recent decades, particularly in the area of political party and interest group participation as discussed in the previous chapter, women candidates still face many barriers in achieving electoral success, including those imposed by the electoral process itself (including incumbency and the reliance on money to fund competitive campaigns), the stereotyping of women candidates during the campaign, and the fact that most women start their political careers later than most male candidates due, in part, to family demands. In addition to the structural impediments, one of the most important barriers for women to overcome is simply making the decision to run for office; the perception for many potential women candidates that they do not have a strong chance of winning, even if untrue, is what contributes to the failure of women "to toss their hats in the ring" and hold more seats in Congress, state legislatures, and eventually the White House.[1]

Yet, a compelling argument can be made as to why more women should become public officeholders and why their leadership at the national, state, and local levels can make an important difference in terms of public policies. Women politicians offer an ideological advantage (regardless of party affiliations, women are often in a better position to address certain societal needs relating to the overall welfare of citizens, or to protest other policies such as war). An increase in women's representation can also help legitimize the political system and provide societal benefits as well with increased competition for public office.[2] In this chapter, we will consider women as political candidates, including the unique challenges that women face in running for office at all levels of government. Breaking into the system to become a political leader is not an easy task for women candidates, particularly given the challenges that women have faced within the party structure and in raising adequate funds to finance campaigns. Also, since the incumbency factor is so prevalent in allowing members of Congress and other elected offices (like legislatures in states without term limits) to hold such a strong advantage in getting reelected, then women and minority candidates often face an uphill battle in reaching some level of parity in terms of representation. There also tends to be a gender bias in news media coverage during campaigns, which can lead to negative stereotyping of women candidates. First, we will look at how women candidates are recruited to run for office, followed by the institutional barriers within the electoral arena with which women candidates must contend, followed by the all-important image created for women candidates through the watchful eyes of the news media.

RECRUITING WOMEN CANDIDATES

Do women receive adequate encouragement and support to run for political office? The initial decision to run is perhaps the most difficult for women to make for their own careers in the short run, yet the most crucial in the longer term goal of placing more women in positions of political power. Although women candidates in the past decade have shown that they can raise money competitively compared to male candidates, and that women can win both congressional and statewide elections, there is still resistance for many potential women candidates to run. According to political scientist Ruth B. Mandel, many young women today have decided to shun the high-pressured, brutally competitive lifestyle that comes with many leadership opportunities, including those within the political arena. As a result, as the number of women in elected positions has leveled off in the past few years (compared to the yearly increases during the early 1990s of percentage of women holding congressional and state positions), many women are thinking twice before committing to becoming a political candidate. Mandel states,

> There is a continuing conundrum here. Nothing will change the picture of leadership and perhaps the practices of leadership unless women themselves choose to pursue leadership. In the United States, far and away, this matter of women's choices stands as the single greatest remaining challenge to achieving parity for women in leadership. . . . They confront more opportunities and options than ever before. Nonetheless, women must choose to walk the path.[3]

Anecdotal evidence about women's political experiences, either while being recruited to run for office or actually running, present a mixed story. Whereas some women report facing hostility at trying to break into a traditionally male-dominated sphere like politics, other women have received tremendous enthusiasm and support from male political elites in their pursuit of public office.[4] Party leaders in both the Democratic and Republican parties during the 1970s and 1980s were not overly committed to recruiting female candidates for Congress. And, when the parties did recruit women, they were often doing little to facilitate their election to office once the campaign began. Patterns emerged in the relationship between female candidates and party leaders to show that contacts between the parties and potential women candidates were less frequent, and women were often recruited to run as "sacrificial lambs" in a district where there was no hope of winning. The reluctance of both the Democratic and Republican parties to "approach women and to present them with the opportunity to run in races [with] at least some chance of general election victory [has been] an important feature of the political opportunity structure that inhibits substantial increases in the numerical representation of women among elective officeholders."[5] More recent analyses that include congressional data into the early 1990s, however, show that women no longer run disproportionately for unwinnable seats and that women are just as likely as men to have party leaders encourage their candidacies.[6]

Women seeking office in state legislatures face similar situations regarding candidate recruitment. The likelihood that a woman will run for a state legislative seat varies from state to state, and ties in with other factors like incumbency, the number of eligible women in the recruitment pool, and the perceived viability of women candidates by party leaders. However, party recruitment can and does play a significant role in electing women legislators in some states. This process often begins at the local level, as local party leaders can provide important information to those candidate gatekeepers at the state level regarding which candidates may have the highest probability of winning an election. Therefore, party leader evaluations of potential candidates play a large role in determining who actually runs for office. According to political scientist Kira Sanbonmatsu, "Where the parties recruit candidates to run or formally or informally support candidates in the primary, party leaders can play a major role in shaping the social composition of the legislature. . . . In states with an organized recruitment process, whether that process yields women candidates very much depends on party leaders' perception of the quality and electability of women candidates and their personal knowledge of or access to names of potential women candidates."[7]

In terms of being eligible to run for political office, most women candidates have the necessary qualifications for the job—most are well educated and have professional or managerial careers (although few tend to be lawyers, perhaps due to the fact that women were in many respects barred from the legal profession until the 1970s). Most women candidates also have some party and organizational experience, although these types of qualifications in general appear to have little effect on election outcomes. Yet, with most political offices still dominated by men, the one qualification that a large number of women still lack is prior officeholding experience. This seemed to represent an important barrier for women candidates, particularly throughout the 1970s and 1980s. According to political scientist Susan J. Carroll, "It is not the case that those who are more qualified win while those who lack qualifications lose. The only variables that seemed to discriminate between winners and losers with any consistency were some measures of party activity and former officeholding."[8] Prior political experience, particularly at the local level, can be a critical indicator of the number of women who will be seen as credible candidates for higher office. Therefore, the "pipeline" or "bottleneck" that allows women to enter the political arena as candidates can explain one of the factors accounting for previous and current shortfalls, since "experience in one elected office is seen as providing credentials for other offices."[9]

Recent studies by political scientists have attempted to better understand the factors that may keep women from running for elected office. Incumbency, as we will discuss in the next section, dominates much of the electoral process in Congress and state legislatures and serves as a structural barrier for all candidates, not just women. Yet there are still specific barriers to elected office that appear to be unique for potential women candidates. The primary reason for women's underrepresentation at all levels of government stems from the simple fact that women choose to run less frequently than men, even though when they are similarly situated to male candidates (in terms of party and financial support) they are just as likely to win. The factors that seem to contribute to a woman's choice not to run include the political gender-role socialization (as discussed in Chapter 3), a lack of political confidence, family responsibilities, and a lack of visible women role models in politics.[10] Also, a critical gender difference exists in the candidate emergence phase due to a substantial winnowing process that yields a smaller ratio of women than men candidates. Women may be less likely to receive encouragement from party officials at this crucial phase, yet women candidates who do choose to run tend to receive similar amounts of support from party leaders and other political activities. Women are also less likely to deem themselves qualified to run for political office, even when they have achieved great professional success. This suggests that "recruitment patterns—or lack thereof—appear to solidify women's self-perceptions."[11]

WOMEN CANDIDATES AND THE ELECTORAL PROCESS

Regardless of the gender of the candidate, the roles incumbency and money play in American political campaigns can explain a lot about who actually gets elected. The incumbency advantage, particularly in Congress, plays the largest role in determining election outcomes. Over time, incumbent members of Congress are reelected in close to 95 percent of races. Sometimes that figure is even higher. In 2002, for example, 98 percent of incumbents in the House of Representatives were reelected. There are many reasons that contribute to the incumbency advantage, including name recognition, the ability to provide services for their constituents (done with the help of congressional staffers) as well as the ability send free mail (known as franking) to voters within their district, the ability to support legislation that their constituents also support, and the advantage over challengers in raising large amounts of money to fund their campaigns. In addition, congressional races receive little news media coverage, which leaves voters uninformed about the candidates and the relevant issues and they instead rely on name recognition or party loyalty when casting a vote. As a result of all these factors combined, challengers tend to be weaker candidates. This is ironic because Americans tend to resoundingly dislike Congress as an institution, yet they never seem to blame their individual representatives for the problems of government waste and legislative gridlock.

Another factor contributing to the incumbency advantage that has become a more pressing problem in recent years is the increasing number of "safe seats." With the help of redistricting, which occurs at the state level, political parties who hold the majority in state legislatures have been able to create safe districts for their members where the opposing party has little or no chance of defeating an incumbent. As a result, nearly one-fourth of all congressional seats in the most recent elections have seen incumbents running unopposed in the general election. This is particularly problematic for women and minority candidates trying to break into the political arena, and explains why both groups, particularly women, tend to do better in open-seat elections where there is no incumbent on the ballot. The incumbency advantage, then, is the most valid explanation for women candidates' lack of greater electoral success. As Carroll points out,

> While incumbents tend to win elections at a much higher rate than nonincumbents, very few women candidates are incumbents. Candidates who run against incumbents (and/or against candidates of the opposing party who have defeated incumbents in primaries) rarely win elections, and sizable numbers of women candidates run in races where they confront such situations.[12]

Women have experienced a higher rate of electoral success in state legislatures due to a higher turnover rate for incumbents, since state legislators are more likely to return to their previous careers or run for higher office, thereby creating more open seats for challengers. (This is also due, in part, to the fact that some states, like Texas, have part-time legislators with low salaries making it difficult to create a long-term career in the state capitol. Other states like California do have full-time, well-paid state legislators, but their time in office is governed by mandatory term limits.)

A 1997 study of women candidates showed that women's success rates were identical to men's when comparing incumbent women and men, when comparing women and men running for open seats, and when comparing female challengers to male challengers. As the authors point out, "the problem for women candidates is not sex but incumbency. Incumbents, most of whom are men, win much more often than challengers. For women to have a level playing field, they have to wait for men to retire, resign, or die, and then run for the open seat."[13] This helps explain the success that women had in 1992, dubbed by the news media as "The Year of the Woman." Several factors contributed to the "extraordinary opportunities for newcomers" in 1992, including an unusually large number of open seats resulting from retirements and redistricting from the 1990 census. American voters were also in a strong anti-incumbent mood following public scandals involving the House post office and bank, which made many incumbents more vulnerable than usual. Women's groups were particularly motivated to nominate and elect women candidates following the Supreme Court confirmation hearings of Clarence Thomas (as discussed in Chapter 5). Seen as a watershed election, women candidates won a record number of seats in both the U.S. House of Representatives and the Senate. In the House, 106 women ran for congressional seats on a major party ticket, and 47 won seats in the general election. In the Senate, 11 women ran and 6 were elected, which contributed to the largest ever one-time increase in candidates and winners. Gains were also made in state legislatures; prior to 1992, women made up 6 percent of Congress and 18 percent of state legislatures, with those numbers increasing to 10 percent in Congress and 20 percent at the state level following the 1992 election.[14]

Money in American politics, and more specifically how to regulate it, has also been a prominent national issue for decades. Since Congress first passed the Federal Election Campaign Act (FECA) in 1971—followed by major amendments to the act in 1974, many Supreme Court rulings, and constant political battles to pass additional legislation limiting the impact of money on campaigns—women candidates have developed effective strategies to raise enough money to fund their campaigns. When the number of women emerging as candidates for political office first started to increase in the 1970s, women struggled to raise adequate campaign funds. Most political observers assumed that because women were underrepresented in both politics (PACs give proportionately more money to incumbents) and the corporate world (where many large single donations come from), women were at a huge disadvantage in terms of fundraising. Most also assumed that potential donors were reluctant to give money to women candidates and that women were "psychologically less predisposed to ask for donations." However, by the 1990s, analyses of campaign funds raised and spent by women candidates showed that women now raise and spend as much or more than their male counterparts.[15] This is, however, an area were incumbents still enjoy a sizable advantage over challengers; regardless of gender, challengers have a harder time raising money because they are often not seen as competitive.

As discussed in Chapter 3, women's political action committees (PACs) have made important financial contributions to women candidates in addition to providing training, consultation, and workers in support of the campaign. The timing of financial contributions also plays an important role as "early money" is seen as crucial for women candidates in securing their party's nomination for the general election. EMILY's List for Democratic pro-choice women candidates, the WISH List for Republican pro-choice women candidates, and the Susan B. Anthony List for Republican pro-life women candidates have provided essential early money to women candidates in recent years. This helps "establish a campaign's viability and signals other contributors" to also give money, and can be crucial for nonincumbent women candidates. However, women's PACs give early money disproportionately to Democratic women candidates for Congress, while Republican women candidates "face a more daunting task of establishing early viability."[16] EMILY's List also pioneered the strategy of "bundling," which is basically the practice of gathering campaign contributions from friends and associates. Donors will write their checks to the candidate's campaign fund, but the bundler takes credit for a large contribution to the campaign while avoiding the Federal Election Commission (FEC) limit on contributions to federal candidates. Based on the most recent campaign finance laws passed in 2002 governing federal elections (which includes congressional campaigns), individuals are limited to contributions of $2,100 per election for the 2005–2006 campaign cycle. Therefore, an individual or PAC can solicit contributions from individuals on behalf of a candidate and then bundle them together to make one large (and legal) contribution to the campaign.

While further analysis of women candidates and fundraising is needed, it has become apparent in recent years that women running for Congress have matched and, at times, outpaced their male counterparts. For example, Senators Barbara Boxer (D) and Dianne Feinstein (D) of California, along with Rep. Jane Harmon (D-CA) and several others are known as prolific fundraisers; Boxer and Feinstein ranked numbers one and two, respectively, in 1992 among top fundraisers for U.S. Senate seats. Two years later, Feinstein raised another $11 million in successfully defending her Senate seat against millionaire Congressional representative Michael Huffington (who spent $30 million on his campaign). In the 1998 congressional elections, 10 of the top 50 fundraisers in the House of Representatives were women candidates, and 11 of the top 50 fundraisers in 2000 were women. Whether or not giving by women to women candidates has contributed to this trend is still somewhat unclear, but fundraising within the women's community (particularly from national women's PACs) has played a significant role in the level of success in this area of campaigning.[17] The recent success among women candidates of both parties for congressional seats may provide an important harbinger for women presidential candidates in the future. While Elizabeth Dole cited a lack of money for her early departure from the Republican presidential primaries in late 1999, the fundraising data from recent congressional campaign cycles "seems to suggest that the traditional economic structural barriers to a woman running for the presidency are beginning to dissipate."[18]

MEDIA COVERAGE
OF WOMEN CANDIDATES

Women politicians have traditionally been viewed by the press as an anomaly—a unique occurrence that deserves attention because it is outside the norm.[19] Trivialization of women in the news media (as discussed in Chapter 3) has also continued, through portrayals on television and in the movies that can lead to "symbolic annihilation" of women in general, as well as the stereotyping that occurs in news coverage of women candidates and politicians.[20] In many campaigns, news media coverage has added to the negative stereotyping of women candidates, thus hurting their efforts to win an elected office. According to political scientist Kim Fridkin Kahn, the news media pay more attention to style over substance when covering female candidates. Since many voters may doubt the policy qualifications of women candidates, news coverage that downplays issues and highlights personal traits develops less favorable images for female candidates. Also, traditionally male issues (the economy, defense, foreign policy) are highlighted during U.S. Senate campaigns, while traditionally female issues (education, health care) are emphasized in gubernatorial races. Kahn suggests that female candidates will have an advantage in discussing these issues, and from the subsequent media coverage, during gubernatorial races, but that women candidates for the Senate should ignore the instinct to alter the accepted male agenda to consider female issues, since "demonstrating their competence in 'male' issues at a time when these issues are salient to the public, women candidates may be able to eradicate potentially damaging sex stereotypes." Women candidates also need to stress typically male traits, such as competence and leadership, during their campaigns.[21]

Other studies have found similar results in the negative stereotyping of women candidates. For example, a study by the White House Project (a nonpartisan organization dedicated to placing more women in top leadership positions within government and business) that included several gubernatorial candidates found that not only did women candidates receive more style coverage rather than that of substance, but that male reporters more often focused on the personal than did female reporters. Also, "reporters were more likely to highlight male candidates' positions and records on the issues and were more likely to quote male candidates' reasoning behind their claims."[22] In a similar study on women candidates in U.S. Senate races, the results showed support for the contention that news media coverage on television "disadvantaged women candidates in the eyes of voters" by providing more favorable coverage of male candidates than of women candidates.[23] However, although these studies and others show that media biases and negative stereotyping of women candidates still exist, "it does appear that coverage is becoming more equitable" with male candidates in terms of quantity and substance.[24]

Much research has been conducted on how the news media portray presidential candidates and how it may or may not impact the outcome of presidential elections, but the role of gender in that electoral area is difficult to determine. Yet, we do know that during Geraldine Ferraro's run for the vice presidency in 1984 (with Democratic nominee Walter Mondale) and Elizabeth Dole's short-lived campaign for the Republican nomination in 1999–2000, gender was a significant label in the news coverage of both women candidates. Studies found that "the most pernicious coverage for both campaigns was the 'lipstick watch,'" with almost 30 percent of Ferraro's coverage and more than 40 percent of Dole's coverage containing references to clothing, makeup, hair, and other feminine categorizations.[25]

According to journalism professor Maria Braden, news coverage of women candidates and women politicians may not be blatantly sexist, but that subtle sex discrimination in the coverage still exists. Our media-saturated political environment demands that image play a large role for both officeholders and office seekers, and it continues to be one of the most pressing problems faced by women running for high public office due to a long-held double standard in the press to

GERALDINE FERRARO AND THE NEWS MEDIA:
A Long and Winding Road

Type in the name Geraldine Ferraro on any Internet search engine, and you will find Web page after Web page that labels her as an "American political leader"[26] or states how she "forever reshaped the American political and social landscape."[27] While many young women today may not be as familiar with Ferraro or her historic run for the vice presidency in 1984, she remains an important symbol in American politics for older generations of women who saw her as a groundbreaking candidate on the national level. The first woman to be nominated on a major party ticket, the congressional member from Queens, New York, would also be the test case for the news media on how to handle a female candidate on the presidential campaign trail.

In her six-year tenure in the House of Representatives, Ferraro gained a reputation for pursuing legislation beneficial to women's causes, including working for passage of the Equal Rights Amendment, sponsoring the Women's Economic Equity Act ending pension discrimination against women, and seeking greater job training and opportunities for displaced homemakers. In 1984, under pressure from women's rights advocates and women's organizations such as NOW to place a woman on the ticket, Democratic presidential nominee Walter Mondale made history by picking Ferraro as his running mate. In spite of her strong reputation as a legislator, Ferraro was considered a gamble by some political analysts, but a necessary one for Mondale to have any chance of upsetting incumbent President Ronald Reagan that November. To Democrats, Ferraro represented the candidate who could close the gender gap—by the summer months of 1983, polls showed that 17 percent fewer women than men supported the president and his policies—making party leaders believe that the powerful voting bloc of women could make the difference. Instead, Reagan walked away with a resounding victory, winning every state except Mondale's home state of Minnesota.

While the race between Mondale and Reagan was never close during the fall months of 1984, Ferraro's presence on the ticket as the "first" woman vice presidential candidate made headlines right up until election day. One of the biggest stories of the campaign became the business dealings of Ferraro's husband, John Zaccaro. When Ferraro revealed that her husband had decided not to release his tax returns because it might compromise his business dealings, the press had a field day. Never before had a candidate's spouse been subjected to such scrutiny by the press. In her book about the campaign, *Ferraro: My Story*, Ferraro recalls stating at a press conference, "He's not the candidate, I am." More than 250 reporters jammed the "disclosure" press conference only to learn that both Ferraro and her husband had overpaid, not underpaid, their federal income taxes.[28] The scrutiny by the press would continue throughout the campaign, on issues ranging from Ferraro's views on abortion as a Catholic (she was pro-choice) to how a "lady" candidate was supposed to act (for example, should she and Mondale hug in public or merely shake hands?) to whether or not, due to her Italian heritage, her family had ties to organized crime (no evidence ever surfaced). Ferraro also recalled that conservative columnist George Will of *The Washington Post* wrote a scathing column about her family finances prior to the press conference at which the tax returns were disclosed. Ferraro challenged him on a national news show, saying he would have to apologize when the tax forms were revealed. Instead, Will sent her a dozen roses with a card that read, "Has anyone told you you are cute when you're mad?"[29]

Throughout the campaign, novel—and somewhat odd—stories about Ferraro kept appearing. Even before the Democratic convention had come to a close, the *Los Angeles Times* ran a "Convention Notebook" column that included an interesting commentary on a new problem Mondale and Ferraro would face: With so many Secret Service agents around, which candidate would go down the elevator first and be forced to wait in the garage for the other? The headline gave away the answer, "During Drafty Delay in a Garage, Protocol Rules It's Ladies First."[30] Many media outlets also could not help but talk about fashion in their political reporting. *The New York Times* story on Ferraro's nomination described her appearance and clothing three separate times: "Mrs. Ferraro, dressed in a white suit, gave the thumbs-up sign in response to the convention" began the second paragraph of the story. Later, the story reported on Ferraro's appearance at a fundraiser earlier in the day, "dressed in a bright turquoise dress," and called Speaker of the House Tip O'Neill's comments about Ferraro "avuncular." The third reference to Ferraro's appearance stated: "Clad in white and wearing a string of pearls about her neck, Mrs. Ferraro bounced in time to the beat of the song, 'New York, New York,' as, with a broad grin, she accepted waves of applause." The news of Ferraro hugging several House colleagues whom she had not seen since Mondale had announced her candidacy was also included in the story.[31] Ferraro's

(continued)

campaign, and resulting relationship with the press, also got off to an auspicious start during an August appearance in Mississippi. Jim Buck Ross, the state agriculture commissioner, quizzed Ferraro on whether or not she could bake blueberry muffins. When she responded "I sure can. Can you?" she was informed that men in the South don't cook. The exchange made headlines for several days in newspapers across the nation.[32]

After the loss in 1984, Ferraro would not return to politics until 1992 when she sought the Democratic nomination in New York for the U.S. Senate. One of four candidates for the nomination, Ferraro believed that much of the press coverage focusing on her novelty as the first woman to run for vice president, and the attacks on her family, were behind her. However, allegations concerning her husband's business connections and questions about their tax returns surfaced again. The stories once again made national headlines, this time mostly due to who was raising the issues—one of her challengers for the nomination, New York comptroller and former member of Congress Elizabeth Holtzman. Like Ferraro, Holtzman was known as a feminist politician supportive of women's rights, and had beaten a veteran incumbent in 1972 to first get elected to Congress. Trailing Ferraro in the early polls, Holtzman went on the attack using negative television ads—like many candidates do—in an attempt to slow down the frontrunner's momentum. But a feminist woman attacking another feminist woman was too good of a story for the national press to pass up, and represented a unique double standard within the news media in that "the women weren't acting the way women were supposed to act" since they were behaving more like male politicians.[33] In the end, neither Ferraro nor Holtzman earned the Democratic nomination, and New York would not participate in the Year of the Woman by sending its first elected woman to the Senate (that would not happen until Hillary Rodham Clinton's election in 2000).

Ferraro again ran unsuccessfully for the U.S. Senate in 1998, losing the Democratic nomination to the eventual winner of the seat, Rep. Charles Schumer. From 1996 to 1998, Ferraro was cohost on the CNN show *Crossfire* as a representative of the political "left," and she continues to provide political commentary as a frequent guest on national television news programs. She, like many others, still waits to see how the second woman nominated for vice president, and eventually president, will be treated by the news media.

insert details about appearance in news stories about women politicians but not in stories about men:

> More than a century later, women politicians are still discovering what [Susan B.] Anthony had learned—that journalists often ask women politicians questions they don't ask men. That reporters describe women politicians in ways and with words that emphasize women's traditional roles and focus on their appearance and behavior. That they perpetuate stereotypes of women politicians as weak, indecisive, and emotional. That they hold women politicians accountable for the actions of their children and husbands, though they rarely hold men to the same standards. . . . When the news media imply that women are anomalies in high public office, the public is likely to regard them as bench warmers rather than as an integral part of government.[34]

Women politicians can also be trivialized by the gender-specific words journalists commonly use to describe them, such as *plucky, spunky,* or *feisty.*[35] Whereas more research on the effects of negative or sexist coverage of women candidates and politicians is needed, particularly as the number of media outlets and types of mediums continue to expand, those studies to date suggest that the news media's portrayal of women as authoritative and legitimate leaders within the political system is sparse. This is a particularly important issue for women candidates to face given the mass media's powerful role in the current political environment.[36]

CONCLUSION

How we elect politicians in the United States plays an important role in determining the number of women who serve in public office. While women candidates, especially when running for Congress, have succeeded in recent years in the area of fundraising, the incumbency advantage still hurts the chances of any new or "outsider" candidates (particularly women and minorities) from winning seats and thereby possibly bringing a different perspective to the policymaking process. Although women officeholders may not be quite the novelty that they once were, negative stereotyping in news coverage of women candidates persists, placing yet another burden on women that they must overcome. In order for more women to be elected to public office, they must be encouraged to do so by political parties and other political activists, and perhaps more important, they need to believe that they have a strong chance of winning, which will encourage more women to enter the eligibility pool. While feminist or pro-choice women candidates made substantial gains in both congressional and state races in 1992, it is worth noting that two years later in 1994 (known as the "Year of the Angry White Male" as the Republican Party captured both houses of Congress for the first time in 40 years), several conservative, pro-life women were also elected to Congress, reminding us that a monolithic view of "women politicians" does not exist. Since the mid-1990s, the gains for women winning elections to public offices at all levels of government have slowed down tremendously with only modest and incremental increases. Perhaps future research by political scientists and other interested observers should continue to consider what changes to both public institutions and public policy result from women at both ends of the political or ideological spectrum running for, and eventually holding, public office.

STUDY/DISCUSSION QUESTIONS

1. What factors contribute to the successful recruitment of women candidates? Why, even with other successful examples, do some women still believe that they cannot win an election?
2. How do party leaders and other political activists impact the recruitment of women candidates? What can they do to encourage more women to run for public office?
3. What role does incumbency play in congressional elections, and why does this serve as such an imposing barrier for women getting elected?
4. Why is early money so important for women candidates, and how have women's PACs helped alleviate this financial burden?
5. In what ways do the news media perpetuate negative stereotypes of both women candidates and women politicians?
6. In more than 20 years since Geraldine Ferraro's historic run for the vice presidency in 1984, why has no other woman been nominated on a major party ticket? Will the next woman vice presidential candidate face similar challenges?

SUGGESTED READINGS

Bystrom, Dianne G., Mary Christine Banwart, Lynda Lee Kaid, and Terry A. Robertson. 2004. *Gender and Candidate Communication: VideoStyle, WebStyle, NewsStyle*. New York: Routledge.

Carroll, Susan J., ed. 2003. *Women and American Politics: New Questions, New Directions*. New York: Oxford University Press.

Carroll, Susan J. 1994. *Women as Candidates in American Politics*, 2nd ed. Bloomington: Indiana University Press.

Darcy, R., Susan Welch, and Janet Clark. 1994. *Women, Elections, and Representation*. Lincoln: University of Nebraska Press.

Kahn, Kim Fridkin. 1996. *The Political Consequences of Being a Woman*. New York: Columbia University Press.

Seltzer, Richard A., Jody Newman, and Melissa Voorhees Leighton. 1997. *Sex as a Political Variable: Women as Candidates & Voters in U.S. Elections*. Boulder, CO: Lynne Rienner

Thomas, Sue, and Clyde Wilcox, eds. 1998. *Women and Elective Office: Past, Present, & Future*. New York: Oxford University Press.

ONLINE RESOURCES

http://www.aim.org/index. Accuracy in Media.
http://www.cmpa.com. The Center for Media and Public Affairs.
http://www.fec.gov. The Federal Election Commission.
http://www.opensecrets.org. OpenSecrets.org.
http://www.dscc.org. Democratic Senatorial Campaign Committee.
http://www.ilsenategop.com/index.htm. Senate Republican Campaign Committee.
http://www.hdcc.org. House Democratic Campaign Committee.

NOTES

1. See Nancy E. McGlen, Karen O'Connor, Laura van Assendelft, and Wendy Gunther-Canada, *Women, Politics, and American Society*, 3rd ed. (New York: Longman, 2002), 92–104.

2. R. Darcy, Susan Welch, and Janet Clark, *Women, Elections, and Representation* (Lincoln: University of Nebraska Press, 1994), 15–18.

3. Ruth B. Mandel, "A Question About Women and the Leadership Option," in *The Difference "Difference" Makes: Women and Leadership*, ed. Deborah L. Rhode, 72 (Stanford, CA: Stanford University Press, 2003).

4. Darcy, Welch, and Clark, *Women, Elections, and Representation*, 27–28.

5. Susan J. Carroll, *Women as Candidates in American Politics*, 2nd ed. (Bloomington: Indiana University Press, 1994), 42–44.

6. Darcy, Welch, and Clark, *Women, Elections, and Representation*, 175–76.

7. Kira Sanbonmatsu, "Candidate Recruitment and Women's Election to the State Legislatures," report prepared for the Center for American Women and Politics, Eagleton Institute of Politics, Rutgers, State University of New Jersey, September 2003.

8. Carroll, *Women as Candidates*, 91.

9. Georgia Duerst-Lahti, "The Bottleneck: Women Becoming Candidates," in *Women and Elective Office: Past, Present, & Future*, ed. Sue Thomas and Clyde Wilcox, 15 (New York: Oxford University Press, 1998).

10. Laurel Elder, "Why Women Don't Run: Explaining Women's Underrepresentation in America's Political Institutions," *Women & Politics* 26, no. 2 (2004): 27–56.

11. Richard L. Fox and Jennifer L. Lawless, "Entering the Arena? Gender and the Decision to Run for Office," *American Journal of Political Science* 48, no. 2 (April 2004): 264–80.

12. Carroll, *Women as Candidates*, 119.

13. Richard A. Seltzer, Jody Newman, and Melissa Voorhees Leighton, *Sex as a Political Variable: Women as Candidates & Voters in U.S. Elections* (Boulder, CO: Lynne Rienner, 1997), 7.

14. Sue Thomas, Introduction in Thomas and Wilcox, *Women and Elective Office*, 6–8.

15. Barbara Burrell, "Campaign Finance: Women's Experience in the Modern Era," in Thomas and Wilcox, *Women and Elective Office*, 26–27.

16. Peter L. Francia, "Early Fundraising by Nonincumbent Female Congressional Candidates: The Importance of Women's PACs," *Women & Politics* 23, no. 1/2 (2001): 7–20.

17. Barbara C. Burrell, "Money and Women's Candidacies for Public Office," in *Women and American Politics: New Questions, New Directions*, ed. Susan J. Carroll, 82 (New York: Oxford University Press, 2003).

18. Victoria A. Farrar–Myers, "A War Chest Full of Susan B. Anthony Dollars: Fund-raising Issues for Female Presidential Candidates," in *Anticipating Madam President*, ed. Robert P. Watson and Ann Gordon, 92 (Boulder, CO: Lynne Rienner, 2003).

19. Patricia Rice, "Women out of the Myths and into Focus," in *Women and the News*, 45–49 (New York: Hastings House, 1978).

20. See Gaye Tuchman, *Hearth and Home: Images of Women in the News* (New York: Oxford University Press, 1978), 7–8; and David L. Paletz, *The Media in American Politics: Contents and Consequences* (New York: Longman, 2002), 135–39.
21. Kim Fridkin Kahn, *The Political Consequences of Being a Woman* (New York: Columbia University Press, 1996), 134–36.
22. Marie C. Wilson, *Closing the Leadership Gap: Why Women Can and Must Help Run the World* (New York: Penguin Books, 2004), 37–38.
23. Martha E. Kropf and John A. Boiney, "The Electoral Glass Ceiling? Gender, Viability, and the News in U.S. Senate Campaigns," *Women & Politics* 23, no. 1/2 (2001): 79–101.
24. Dianne G. Bystrom, Mary Christine Banwart, Lynda Lee Kaid, and Terry A. Robertson, *Gender and Candidate Communication: VideoStyle, WebStyle, NewsStyle* (New York: Routledge, 2004), 21.
25. Diane J. Heith, "The Lipstick Watch: Media Coverage, Gender, and Presidential Campaigns," in Watson and Gordon, *Anticipating Madam President*, 124–26.
26. "Geraldine Anne Ferraro," *infoplease,* accessed at http://www.infoplease.com/ce6/people/A0818528.html.
27. "Geraldine Ferraro: Women of the Hall," *National Women's Hall of Fame,* accessed at http://www.greatwomen.org/women.php?action=viewone&id=61.
28. Geraldine A. Ferraro and Linda Francke, *Ferraro: My Story* (New York: Bantam Books, 1985), 174–80.
29. Ibid., 179–80.
30. "Convention Notebook: During Drafty Delay in a Garage, Protocol Rules It's Ladies First," *Los Angeles Times,* July 20, 1984, p. A7.
31. Jane Perlez, "'Gerry, Gerry,' the Convention Chants," *The New York Times,* July 20, 1984, p. A1.
32. Bernard Weinraub, "Mississippi Farm Topic: Does She Bake Muffins?" *The New York Times,* August 2, 1984, p. 16.
33. Braden, *Women Politicians,* 134.
34. See Maria Braden, *Women Politicians and the Media* (Lexington: University Press of Kentucky, 1996), 1–4.
35. Ibid., 6–7.
36. Kim Fridkin Kahn, "Assessing the Media's Impact on the Political Fortunes of Women," in Carroll, *Women and American Politics,* 173–89.

CHAPTER 5

Women as Legislators

Some things will still be unfinished when you die. But if you keep at it and lay the foundation and bring others in, they'll carry on.

—U.S. Senator Dianne Feinstein (D-CA)

*I*n recent years, women have made great strides in getting elected to legislative positions, both at the federal and state level. These seats of power within the American system of government represent a crucial aspect of policymaking as legislators are directly responsible for writing the laws at all levels of government. There are now more women serving in the U.S. Congress and in state legislatures across the country than ever before. At the start of the 109th Session of Congress in 2005, three states (California, Maine, and Washington) held the distinction of being represented by two women in the U.S. Senate, an institution long regarded as an exclusive all-male club in Washington, DC. In the House of Representatives, Nancy Pelosi (D-CA) made history in 2003 with her election to the top Democratic leadership post as House Minority Leader, the highest leadership position in Congress ever held by a woman.

But despite the progress in the past decade or so, women are still nowhere close to reaching parity with men as members of Congress or state legislators. As discussed in Chapter 1, women still make up only about 15 percent of Congress and 22.5 percent of state legislatures. This serves as an important paradox for women, who make up 51 percent of the voting population—how to translate that voting strength into proportional representation within state and national government. Why such slow progress in getting women elected to legislative positions? And when women do get elected to office, why do so few rise to leadership positions within the party ranks? As we discussed in Chapter 4 and will continue to discuss here, women have traditionally faced unique barriers during their pursuit of legislative careers. Another important question to consider concerns the leadership style of women legislators, and whether or not they make a difference in terms of both the policymaking process and policy outcomes. In this chapter, we will discuss women and legislative leadership, the history of women serving in Congress, the impact of women legislators on the policy agenda, and the number and impact of women serving in state legislatures.

WOMEN AND LEGISLATIVE LEADERSHIP

Why study women as legislators, and what can we learn about women's style of leadership in this political venue? First, it is important to understand how a legislature functions to achieve its ultimate goal of lawmaking. Individual members of a legislature are elected to represent an equal number of citizens (or in the case of the U.S. Senate, states are represented equally with two members each) in the policymaking process. While some members may have more seniority or may be members of the majority party, which may in turn provide them more powerful committee or leadership positions, all legislatures within the United States operate on the simple premise of "one person, one vote." In most areas of the decision-making process, a simple majority among the members in both houses is required to pass a bill that will then be sent to the executive branch to be signed or vetoed by the president or state governor. (Exceptions in Congress include, for example, a two-thirds vote to override a presidential veto, or to approve a constitutional amendment to then be considered by the states.) As a result, consensus building and cooperation among members is necessary to pass legislation.

Cindy Simon Rosenthal, in her study of women state legislators, explains that the study of legislative leadership has mostly considered men and as a result has failed to acknowledge the contribution of women to lawmaking in recent decades. "Congressional studies, which dominate the legislative literature, remain mostly about men. Might it be that male behavior has been conflated as institutional behavior?"[1] If women traditionally exhibit leadership traits that are more openly democratic, cooperative, and promote a group-centered mode for decision making, then one might assume that women have had a positive impact on how legislatures function.

Rosenthal's study, which consisted of surveys of legislative committee chairs from 50 states, focus groups, interviews, and an extensive study of the state legislatures in Colorado, Ohio, and Oklahoma, demonstrated that "sex, the social understandings of gender, and gendered institutions all influence leadership style."[2] She categorizes legislative leadership as two distinct styles: aggregative (also known as transactional—a style that is leader-centered, hierarchical, with leaders exercising power over others) and integrative (also known as transformational—a style that is nonhierarchical and one that stresses mutuality and community, empowering others, and a common purpose among members).[3] Aggregative or transactional leadership is considered to be the norm within legislatures or in part due to the study of institutions as historically dominated by men. However, the integrative or transformational leadership style has also been present in legislatures as women have gained a more prominent role, yet researchers have mostly ignored this until very recently. By examining institutions in which both men and women occupy leadership roles, modest differences in leadership traits among men and women become apparent. For example, women committee chairs often exhibit leadership styles closer to the integrative-transformational model. As Rosenthal concludes, "Leadership is a complex phenomenon of individual experiences, circumstances, and relationships. Nonetheless, on a wide variety of individual measures of leadership traits, motivation, or behavior, women and men differ in ways that are substantively and statistically significant."[4]

WOMEN IN CONGRESS: A HISTORY

Since the founding of the nation in 1776, nearly 12,000 people have served in the national legislature (the Continental Congress from 1776 to 1787, followed by the current U.S. Congress). Of those, only 1.8 percent have been women.[5] The main argument put forth by suffragists in the struggle to secure the vote for women centered on the argument that women should not be prevented from civic participation and duties, and that women should be allowed to select their own representatives. So when women did secure the right to vote with the ratification of the Nineteenth Amendment to the U.S. Constitution in 1920, many assumed that women would voice their political preferences by electing other women. However, as discussed in Chapter 3, not all women rushed to the ballot box to participate in the electoral process. Other factors came in to play as well to contribute to the many obstacles that women politicians would face in the following decades. Few women actually sought elective office during the first half of the twentieth century, and of those who did, several were nominated by the minority party in a particular district where the candidate had little chance of winning.

The first woman to serve in the U.S. Congress was actually elected before women nationwide had the right to vote. Jeannette Rankin, a Republican from Montana, served two terms in the U.S. House of Representatives, the first from 1917 to 1918 (Montana had granted women's suffrage prior to 1920) and the second from 1941 to 1942. Rankin, a pacifist, was the only member of Congress to vote against American entry into both World War I and World War II. Rebecca Latimer Felton, a Georgia Democrat in her 80s, became the first woman to serve in the U.S. Senate in 1922. She was appointed as a temporary replacement to a vacant seat, and served for only two days before giving up her seat to the man who had been elected to it. Hattie Wyatt Caraway, an Arkansas Democrat who was appointed to the U.S Senate to succeed her late husband in 1931, was the first of many women to take this path to the Senate. After her appointment to the office, Caraway would later become the first woman ever elected to the Senate in her own right, where she served two full terms. She was also the first woman to chair a Senate committee— the minor position of chair of the Committee on Enrolled Bills.

While women succeeding to the Congress as widows was a common occurrence throughout the twentieth century, it is now more often the exception than the rule. When a vacancy occurs in the House of Representatives, a special election must be held. As such, a widow has the advantage of name recognition. In the Senate, a vacancy is usually filled through a gubernatorial appointment until the next regularly scheduled federal election (which occurs every even-numbered year). However, three more recent examples show that this practice is still in effect. Doris Matsui, widow of 26-year House veteran Robert Matsui, won a special election to her late husband's district in California in March 2005. Mary Bono, the widow of entertainer and former Palm Springs, California, mayor Sonny Bono, won a special election to fill his House seat upon his accidental death in 1998. And in the Senate, Jean Carnahan represented the state of Missouri for two years after her husband posthumously won the election in 2002. Mel Carnahan, a Democrat, died in a plane crash two weeks prior to the election, where he was challenging the incumbent Republican Senator John Ashcroft. His wife Jean was then appointed to fill the Senate seat by the state governor, but she lost her reelection bid in 2004.

Major growth in the number of women seeking legislative office at the national level, and as a result women being elected to office, did not occur until the late 1960s and early 1970s. The modern women's movement began to change the political environment, albeit slowly, which encouraged more women to seek political office in an effort to change public policies that affected them directly. One woman who arrived in Congress during this time period was Patricia Schroeder, who served 24 years in the House of Representatives as a Democrat from Colorado. Schroeder was elected to Congress in 1972 at the age of 32. Her first campaign, run out of her own house, focused on ideas rather than on money. She also beat the political odds to win the seat, since her campaign was also short on political support and endorsements. The only endorsements she received came from the few African American elected officials in Colorado at the time. Not only did the Democratic Party refuse to support her campaign, but the Colorado Women's Political Caucus, which she had helped found, also denied her an endorsement. The average campaign contribution was a mere $7.50, which came from several individual supporters within the congressional district.[6] Schroeder, who defied the critics and naysayers when she first got elected, always maintained a leadership style focused on her outsider status, as opposed to the many women she would later see in Congress who tried to move things along and play by the rules: "It's not that they lack vision, but they want to remain players. Whereas I arrived realizing I would *never* be a player—so I would play the outsider game."[7]

By 1984, the number of women nominated by their party to run for the House of Representatives had increased dramatically. That same year U.S. Representative Geraldine Ferraro of New York became Democrat Walter Mondale's running mate in the presidential election. A total of 65 women ran for the House that year; however, only 22 women were elected, and most who won were incumbents. Many political watchers concluded that while Ferraro's candidacy had been symbolic for women, real progress in the number of women elected had not occurred.

In 1986, Barbara Mikulski of Maryland became the first Democratic woman elected to the Senate without first being appointed to the seat. Mikulski, who is now known as a master strategist in getting bills passed, spent her early years in the Senate learning as much about the institution and its processes as possible. She also respected the Senate traditions and rules, and sought the guidance and advice of the Democratic men with whom she served:

> I was at an initial disadvantage as a woman coming to the Senate, and it wasn't just that the gym was off-limits. I didn't come to politics by the traditional male route, being in a nice law firm or belonging to the right clubs. Like most of the women I've known in politics, I got involved because I saw a community need. And it was tough, absolutely. I didn't have any natural mentors to show me the ropes. I had to seek out my mentors. So when four women finally

joined me in the Senate in 1993, I was very gratified. I gladly took on the role of mentor and adviser.[8]

A nomination to the U.S. Supreme Court in the fall of 1991 would serve as a catalyst for more women running for office, more women getting elected, and the start of a grassroots effort among women's advocacy groups to change the gender balance on Capitol Hill. When President George H. W. Bush nominated Clarence Thomas to fill a vacancy on the Supreme Court due to the retirement of Associate Justice Thurgood Marshall, no one could have predicted the national firestorm over sexual harassment that would be unleashed. When law professor Anita Hill's claims of sexual harassment against Thomas, for whom she had worked at the Equal Employment Opportunity Commission, were leaked to the press, Hill was called to testify before the all-male Senate Judiciary Committee. Prior to the Senate investigation into the charges, it was unclear as to whether the Senate would take the accusations seriously.

Seven women in the House of Representatives were outraged over the apparent indifference to such a charge by their male colleagues in the Senate. On October 8, 1991, the women, led by Schroeder and including then member of the House Barbara Boxer (D-CA), Louise Slaughter (D-NY), Eleanor Holmes-Norton (D-DC), Nita Lowey (D-NY), Patsy Mink (D-HI), and Jolene Unsoeld (D-WA), along with several reporters in tow, marched up the steps to the Senate on the opposite side of the Capitol to demand that their concerns be heard by the Democratic leadership. Boxer recalled later that the women wanted to help Democratic senators, who were attending their regular Tuesday Democratic caucus lunch, understand the importance of the issue. At the time, only two women (Mikulski and Nancy Kassebaum, a Republican from Kansas) were serving in the Senate. The women believed that their perspective would be welcomed; instead, they initially found themselves outside a closed door where they were not allowed to enter. Finally, with the threat of negative press coverage from the reporters present, Senate Majority Leader George Mitchell agreed to meet with the women in a side room.

Further testimony and investigations did follow into Hill's allegations against Thomas. However, Thomas was confirmed by the full Senate in a vote of 52–48 (the second closest vote ever to confirm a Supreme Court nominee). More important, for many women across the nation, the event proved to be galvanizing in the sense that women were not a visible part of the political elite within Washington. Boxer recalled, "It was humiliating to be so summarily dismissed—to have to beg for a hearing. But we kept demanding to be heard until [Mitchell] agreed to meet with us. And so we got our hearing. It turned out to be a travesty. It was shameful. But it was also a wake-up call. All over the country, women watched those hearings, and reacted to seeing that long row of white male senators. It was made painfully clear that they just 'didn't get it.'"[9]

As a result, the presidential and congressional election year of 1992 became known as The Year of the Woman. Many more women ran for Congress than in years past due in part to the Hill—Thomas controversy. As a result, the number of women in Congress rose from 32 at the end of the 102nd Congress to 52 during the 103rd Congress, including 20 new women members in the House and 4 new women senators. (The new senators included Democrats Barbara Boxer and Dianne Feinstein of California, Patty Murray of Washington, and Carol Moseley Braun of Illinois; Republican Kay Bailey Hutchison of Texas increased the number to seven when she won a special election in June 1993 to replace Democrat Lloyd Bentsen who had been appointed treasury secretary in the new Clinton administration.) More than 60 million women had voted in the general election in November 1992, which played a crucial role in the largest increase in the number of women elected to Congress in history. The success of women candidates in 1992 can also be attributed to many other factors, including redistricting, a record number of retirements from the House in 1992, and the House post office scandal in 1991 and the House bank scandal in 1992. These issues, as well as legislative gridlock between a Democratic-controlled Congress and a Republican White House, contributed to the public desire in 1992 for a change in the membership and policies on Capitol Hill. Women capitalized on this situation as relative newcomers; "with a strong reputation for honesty and integrity on the one hand, and expertise on many domestic issues on the other, women were looked upon to initiate reform."[10]

Since 1992, the number of women serving in Congress has steadily yet slowly increased. As of June 2005, there are currently a total of 80 women serving in Congress—66 in the House and 14 in the Senate (see Table 5.1 for the current women members of the Senate). Twenty-six states are now represented by at least one woman in the House. Among the largest states, California has 18 women representatives, New York has 6, and Florida has 5. Texas, now the second most populous state in the nation, has only 3 women in its House delegation (see Table 5.2). Of the 80 women currently serving in Congress, a total of 20 (25 percent) are women of color, and 10 of those women are members of the California House delegation (the most populous state in the nation with the greatest racial and ethnic diversity among its citizens).

TABLE 5.1 Women in the 109th Congress—U.S. Senate

Senator	State (Party Affiliation)	Year Elected
Barbara Boxer	California (D)	1992
Maria Cantwell	Washington (D)	2000
Hillary Rodham Clinton	New York (D)	2000
Susan Collins	Maine (R)	1996
Elizabeth Dole	North Carolina (R)	2002
Dianne Feinstein	California (D)	1992
Kay Bailey Hutchison	Texas (R)	1993
Mary Landrieu	Louisiana (D)	1996
Blanche Lincoln	Arkansas (D)	1998
Barbara Mikulski	Maryland (D)	1986
Lisa Murkowski	Alaska (R)	2002
Patty Murray	Washington (D)	1992
Olympia Snowe	Maine (R)	1994
Debbie Stabenow	Michigan (D)	2000

Source: Center for American Women and Politics, Rutgers, State University of New Jersey.

TABLE 5.2 Women in the 109th Congress—U.S. House of Representatives

State	# Women Representatives Total Represanatives	Percentage
California	19/53	33.9%
Colorado	2/7	28.6
Connecticut	2/5	40.0
Florida	5/25	20.0
Georgia	1/13	7.7
Illinois	3/19	15.8
Indiana	1/9	11.1
Kentucky	1/6	16.7
Michigan	2/15	13.3
Minnesota	1/8	12.5
Missouri	1/9	11.1
New Mexico	1/3	33.3
New York	6/29	20.7
Nevada	1/3	33.3
North Carolina	2/13	15.4
Ohio	3/18	16.7
Oregon	1/5	20.0
Pennsylvania	2/19	10.5
South Dakota	1/1	100
Tennessee	1/9	11.1
Texas	3/32	9.4
Virginia	2/11	18.2
Washington	1/9	11.1
West Virginia	1/3	33.3
Wisconsin	2/8	25.0
Wyoming	1/1	100

Source: Center for American Women and Politics, Rutgers, State University of New Jersey.

CONGRESSIONAL REPRESENTATIVE
LORETTA SANCHEZ:

Playing by Her Own Rules

Rep. Loretta Sanchez (D-CA) knows how to make headlines. A political novice when she ran for the House of Representatives in 1996, she defeated an 18-year House veteran, the outspoken archconservative icon Robert Dornan, by a mere 984 votes. Dornan would not leave his seat quietly, accusing the Sanchez campaign of "cheating" by relying on the illegal votes of nonresident immigrants. A House investigation proved otherwise, and after lots of press attention on both the local and national level, Sanchez' political career had begun. In 1998, Sanchez handily beat Dornan in a rematch by 17 percent of the votes. In 2000, as co-chair of the Democratic National Committee, Sanchez' plans to host a fundraiser at the Playboy mansion in Los Angeles during the Democratic National Convention upset many party leaders (at first refusing to relocate the fundraiser, Sanchez eventually changed her venue). In April 2001, while many of her congressional colleagues were postponing or canceling trips to China during the U.S. spy plane standoff, Sanchez went ahead with the visit with about a dozen other U.S. lawmakers. In 2003, Sanchez made history when her sister, Linda Sanchez, was also elected to the House of Representatives from California, making them the first sisters and the first women of any relation to ever serve in Congress.

Sanchez represents the 47th Congressional District of California, which includes the cities of Anaheim, Garden Grove, Santa Ana, and some of Fullerton in Orange County. Raised in Anaheim by immigrant parents from Mexico and one of seven children, Sanchez never intended to pursue a political career. She earned a bachelor's degree in 1982 in economics from Chapman University in Orange, California (where she was voted "Business Student of the Year"), and then earned an MBA from American University in Washington, DC. She then began a business career as a financial manager at the Orange County Transportation Authority, followed by consulting work, including a position at Booz, Allen and Hamilton, one of the top consulting firms in the nation. Sanchez then started her own consulting business in Santa Ana, California, assisting public agencies and private firms with financial matters, including cost–benefit analysis, strategic planning, and capital acquisition.[11]

However, when the opportunity presented itself to run for the House in 1996 to represent the community in which she grew up,

Sanchez relied on determination and a strong grassroots effort to win both the Democratic primary and the general election. The changing demographics in Orange County helped as well. Long known as a conservative Republican stronghold, the mostly upscale county south of Los Angeles on the California coastline had grown from a population of 400,000 to 2.8 million during the 1990s. In addition, Republican voter registration dropped from 55 to 49 percent during that time period, due in part to the loss of many middle-class aerospace jobs and a large wave of Latino/Latina and Asian immigrants who tended to vote Democratic. Sanchez' upset victory over Dornan in 1996 proved the point that Orange County was no longer dominated by its "reliably rock-solid, conservative, suburban, white, Republican vote—the kind of vote you could take to the bank, and which scores of [Republican] candidates did."[12]

Her supporters have called Sanchez a "dragon slayer" and a "modern-day Helen of Troy," not only for her upset victory over Dornan in 1996, but due to her tenaciousness and independence in representing her constituents.[13] A former Republican, she has been known to side with Republican colleagues on issues dealing with the economy or national security. Sanchez is the ranking woman on the House Armed Services Committee, and was selected by Democratic leader Nancy Pelosi to serve as the second-ranking Democrat on the House Committee on Homeland Security. She is also a member of the Hispanic Caucus, the Women's Congressional Caucus, the Blue Dog Democrats (a group of fiscally conservative House Democrats who tend to vote together as a coalition on budgetary and economic issues), the New Democratic Coalition (known as the moderate or centrist, as opposed to liberal, wing of the Democratic Party), and the Congressional Human Rights Caucus.

Sanchez' leadership style focuses on community involvement and accessibility to constituents within her district. She travels home each week from Washington to regularly hold what she calls "Community Office Hours" to meet with constituents and generate community interest in key government issues. In 2002, Sanchez was selected to serve as Chapman University's first Latina member of the Board of Trustees. As for future political aspirations, Sanchez has hinted that she may be interested in running for the U.S. Senate, and even considered running for California governor when voters recalled incumbent Democrat Gray Davis in 2003. Regardless of what options may be in her political future—a statewide position in California or even higher—Sanchez has already proved herself as a force to be reckoned with in the political arena.

WOMEN IN CONGRESS:
THE POLICY AGENDA

Studies in the past decade have shown that having more women serve in state legislatures, as well as their visibility within the institution (leadership positions, access to the news media, etc.) can positively impact the success of legislation that affects women.[14] However, not all women in the Congress are homogeneous, either in terms of style or the substance of their policy agendas. Yet, most women members of Congress "perceive of themselves as surrogate representatives for women and share some common perceptions about the experiences and ties that bind women together," even though they differ in their party affiliation, political ideologies, racial and ethnic backgrounds, and in the districts or states they represent.[15] As Senator Olympia Snowe points out, the women in the Senate are all different "in our political positions, our styles, our life experiences. However, women just come from a different place than men do in terms of being more relationship-oriented and more collaborative. In fact, many of the skills women develop in life actually work pretty well in this institution . . . where collaboration is an essential ingredient in getting things done."[16] Despite partisan affiliations, most women in the Congress have forged a sense of collegiality that comes from their experiences as women in a traditionally male-dominated institution. The women in the Senate, for example, get together for regular informal dinners in Washington. The purpose of the dinners is not behind-the-scenes deal making, but serves as a "familiar ritual among women colleagues everywhere—that uniquely female manner of lending support by sharing experiences, describing challenges, and talking about the issues they care about."[17]

The women in the House of Representatives have a more formal method of discussing important issues and collaborating on pieces of legislation dealing with women's issues. The Congressional Caucus for Women's Issues, a bipartisan group founded in 1977, has fought for passage of many bills dealing with economic, educational, and health care issues, among others. One of the biggest challenges the caucus has ever faced came in 1995, when Republicans gained control of both houses of Congress for the first time in 40 years. With a commitment to reduce the cost and size of government, the Republican leadership eliminated all legislative service organizations (which included the women's caucus). Such organizations could still exist, but were to be renamed congressional member organizations and would no longer receive public funding to pay for office space and staff. As a result, the co-chairs of the organization (one woman from each party) now take on the responsibilities of the caucus in addition to their regular duties as a member of the House.

Most, but not all, women in the House are members, and legislative priorities that became laws in recent years have included: stronger child care funding and child-support provisions as part of the welfare reforms in 1996; increased spending for and the eventual reauthorization of the Violence Against Women Act programs; contraceptive coverage for women participating in the Federal Employee Health Benefits Program; Medicaid coverage for low-income women diagnosed with breast cancer; bills to strengthen stalking, sex offender, and date rape laws; as well as many other pieces of legislation dealing with women's issues. With the exception of a few years during the 1990s, the bipartisan membership of the caucus has agreed to take a neutral stand on the issue of abortion to keep the organization more inclusive. The caucus also continues to pursue alliances with women senators, as well as the House and Senate leadership in both parties, other caucuses, and the White House. While more than 200 caucuses have existed in the House in recent years focusing on a variety of policy issues, the women's caucus has remained (along with the Congressional Black Caucus) as one of the most resilient and successful caucuses. In order for the caucus to continue to succeed, it must "celebrate its diversity while channeling the tremendous energy and talent of the growing membership into concrete legislative action."[18]

WOMEN IN STATE LEGISLATURES

Historically, state legislatures have served as an important political opportunity for women, and it has been at the state level that women have come closest to achieving parity with men in terms of representation. Women began to make substantial progress during the 1970s in getting elected to state legislatures, and that progress continued through the 1990s. When serving in leadership positions in state legislatures, women tend to differ from their male colleagues in important ways, namely that they "approach politics with an understanding and skills that have been shaped by family, community, volunteerism, and education. . . . Women are older, defer political careers until past their primary years of childrearing and family responsibilities, and hone their leadership ability in the classroom and community center rather

CONGRESSIONAL LEADERSHIP:
One More Glass Ceiling Broken

In 1925, Rep. Mae Ella Nolan (R-CA) became the first woman to chair a congressional committee when, during the 68th Congress, she chaired the Committee on Expenditures in the Post Office Department. Nearly eight decades later, another representative from California, Democrat Nancy Pelosi, became the highest-ranking women to ever hold a leadership position when her Democratic colleagues supported her as the House Minority Leader prior to the start of the 108th Congress. While more women than ever before are now serving in Congress, the top leadership positions in Congress have remained an important glass ceiling for women in politics. Pelosi served as the Democratic whip, the number two leadership position for the minority party, prior to her ascension to Democratic leader.

Why are leadership posts so important within Congress? As a political institution, Congress is dominated by party politics. The U.S. Constitution maintains our two-party system of government with single-member congressional districts. That means that in order to win a congressional seat, a candidate needs a simple majority (or plurality if more than two candidates are on the ballot) to win the seat and represent all citizens within the district. The difficulty in a third-party candidate winning the majority of votes in a congressional district preserves the two-party system. As a result, the two major parties—Democrats and Republicans—control the rules that govern the policymaking process within Congress.

In the House of Representatives, the Speaker of the House comes from the majority party. The Speaker refers bills to committees, appoints members to special committees, and grants members the right to speak during debates. After the Speaker, the top leadership posts in the House include the majority leader and whip, and the minority leader and whip. The party leaders and whips try to organize their members to support or oppose legislative proposals. Whips are usually selected from among the most experienced members of the House. Majority party members also chair and hold a majority of seats on the House's standing committees and subcommittees. The Senate is similar with positions of majority and minority leaders and whips, but does not have a speaker.

Since taking over the position as House minority leader in 2003, Pelosi has earned a reputation as a pragmatic leader who is not afraid to speak her mind in public. Since first elected to the House in 1987, she has also been known as a top Democratic fundraiser and policy strategist. However, the Democrats' choice of Pelosi for the top leadership position in the House was questioned by many political commentators, even those sympathetic to the party's policy positions, due to her image as a San Francisco liberal. She took over the job from Richard Gephardt, a more centrist Democrat from Missouri, but her voting record seems to be in line with a majority of House Democrats, even if it does not represent the views of mainstream Democratic voters nationwide.[19] While moderate Democrats preferred the leadership style of Gephardt, who was always careful not to offend anyone with his positions, liberals within the party like Pelosi's style of "coming out swinging" with clear positions for the Democratic Party. In May 2004, frustrated by the Bush administration's policies in the war in Iraq, she criticized President George W. Bush by saying, "I believe that the president's leadership and the actions taken in Iraq demonstrate an incompetence in terms of knowledge, judgment and experience."

Pelosi, who has five children, did not seek elective office until her children were mostly grown. Her father, Thomas J. D'Alesandro Jr., was a former member of Congress and mayor of Baltimore. Pelosi has been quite candid with the press about her intention to help the Democrats regain control of the House so that she can become the first woman Speaker. She has been called an "elegant and energetic" politician who has "the kind of star quality that many say makes them again excited to be Democrats. Young women come to the Capitol to have their picture taken in front of her office. Donations to the Democratic Congressional Campaign Committee have increased by 30 percent, officials there say, since her signature began appearing on the direct mail."[20] Whether or not Pelosi will move into the Speaker's office on Capitol Hill remains to be seen, but she has nonetheless broken an important glass ceiling for women in Congress as the first woman to lead her party.

than in the boardroom and locker room."[21] Women also engage in different legislative activities than men, including spending more time on constituent concerns, building coalitions both within and across party lines, and studying proposed legislation, making "women appear to be better team players with the legislature than are men." However, women legislators spend equal amounts of time as men do on traditional legislative activities such as campaigning, fundraising, seeking pork-barrel legislation (which brings state funds home to their district), and introducing new legislation.[22]

Research in recent years has also shown that in general, women legislators at the state level serve as "agents of policy-related change" in representing those constituents who are economically disadvantaged, changing expenditure priorities for their state, and conducting business in public as opposed to the old-style backroom political negotiations. Women legislators have also given more priority than their male colleagues to legislation dealing with health care, welfare issues concerning families and children, and in promoting policies to help other women;[23] women legislators are also more liberal across the board than their male colleagues regardless of partisan affiliation.[24] As the number of women in state legislatures has grown in recent decades, and as women legislators have worked together through political caucuses, they have been able to move issues of greatest concern to women (like family leave, domestic violence, and comparable worth) into the legislative mainstream of state policy agendas.[25]

State legislatures represent an important function for women in politics for several reasons. First, state legislatures are an important entry point for women who seek higher political office. Second, the rate of gains for women at the state level directly impacts the percentage of women serving in the Congress and in other executive branch positions. And third, state legislatures decide many of the policy issues that are historically of direct concern to women (like education, health care, workplace policies, etc.).[26] Like their counterparts in Congress, many women in state legislatures pay considerable attention to domestic and women's issues, yet as a group, their policy choices are diverse and they do not represent a voting bloc committed to women's issues alone.[27] Historically, legislative sessions were scheduled to accommodate the schedules and economic responsibilities of men, including the cycles of planting, growing, and harvesting crops when the nation had a primarily agricultural economy. Based on the tradition that legislatures were run by men, the legislative schedule can still create a burden for women, who "experience the schedule of legislative life differently. . . . Even in contemporary times, as women participate in larger numbers in the paid labor force, the weight of household obligations continues to discourage women from legislative service. Women legislators are significantly more likely to serve in districts that are closer to the state capital, commuting daily to balance public and private duties."[28]

The first women to serve as state legislators were elected prior to the turn of the twentieth century. In 1894, three women—Clara Cressingham, Carrie C. Holly, and Frances Klock—were elected to the Colorado House of Representatives, the first women elected to any state legislature. Two years later in 1896, Martha Hughes Cannon was elected to the Utah State Senate, becoming the first woman state senator. More than a century later, many more women have followed in the paths of these early women politicians. In 2004, 1,661 (22.5 percent) of the 7,382 state legislators in the United States were women (women held 412, or 20.9 percent, of the 1,971 state senate seats and 1,249, or 23.1 percent, of the 5,411 state house or assembly seats). Since 1971, the number of women serving in state legislatures has increased more than fourfold. Of the women state legislators serving in 2004, nearly one-fifth (18.4 percent) were women of color.[29]

In the last few years, however, progress has slowed a bit in electing women to state political positions in all three branches of government—legislative, executive, and judicial. The number of women in state elective office has leveled off nationwide. Not many clear patterns exist across states to explain the number of women serving in state legislatures. However, two trends do emerge: A majority of women legislators are Democrats, and states in the South lag behind other states in electing women to state legislatures. Democratic women outnumber Republican women in state legislatures in spite of a nationwide voting trend in the past decade of more Republicans being elected than Democrats. Of all women state senators, 63.2 percent are Democrats, and of all women state representatives, 59.6 are Democrats. As for southern states and the dearth of women legislators, Table 5.3 shows that many of the states with the smallest percentage of women legislators are found in this region of the country. Only one southern state—Florida—has remained competitive with other top-ranked states in electing women to state legislative office.[30]

Beginning in the 1990s, women began to make substantial progress in holding state legislative leadership positions. Through the end of 2003, 20 women (6 Democrats and 14 Republicans) in 14 states had served as speakers and 9 women (3 Democrats and 6 Republicans) in 7 states had served as senate presidents. When all leadership

TABLE 5.3 Women in State Legislatures, 2005

State	Number and Percentage of Women in State Legislature	
Alabama	14/140	10.0%
Alaska	11/60	18.3
Arizona	30/90	33.3
Arkansas	22/135	16.3
California	37/120	30.8
Colorado	33/100	33.0
Connecticut	54/187	28.9
Delaware	21/62	33.9
Florida	29/120	23.8
Georgia	36/180	18.2
Hawaii	21/76	27.6
Idaho	29/105	27.6
Illinois	50/177	28.2
Indiana	25/150	16.7
Iowa	30/150	20.0
Kansas	54/165	32.7
Kentucky	17/138	12.3
Louisiana	23/144	16.0
Maine	44/186	23.7
Maryland	64/188	34.0
Massachusetts	49/200	24.5
Michigan	30/148	20.3
Minnesota	60/201	29.9
Mississippi	22/174	12.6
Missouri	42/197	21.3
Montana	37/150	24.7

positions, and not just the top posts, are considered, the percentages for women serving are even stronger. Through 2003, a total of 46 (13.6 percent) of all leadership positions in state legislatures were held by women, and women also chaired a total of 346 (18.9 percent) of all standing committees in state legislatures. A strong relationship exists between states electing more women to state legislatures and those same states placing more women in positions of leadership, either as party leaders or committee chairs.[31] A "feminization" of state legislative leadership has also occurred. Not only has the increased number of women legislators led to more women holding leadership positions, but a more "feminine" leadership style that emphasizes consensus and compromise has emerged for both women *and* men in leadership positions.[32] Women have also capitalized on legislative power through holding committee chairs, which emphasizes "getting the job done" in terms of passing legislation as opposed to posi-

State	Number and Percentage of Women in State Legislature	
Nebraska	12/49	24.5
Nevada	21/63	33.3
New Hampshire	130/424	30.7
New Jersey	19/120	15.8
New Mexico	35/112	31.3
New York	50/212	23.6
North Carolina	39/170	22.9
North Dakota	23/141	16.3
Ohio	26/132	19.7
Oklahoma	22/149	14.8
Oregon	26/90	28.9
Pennsylvania	32/253	12.6
Rhode Island	19/113	16.8
South Carolina	15/170	8.8
South Dakota	17/105	16.2
Tennessee	23/132	17.4
Texas	36/181	19.9
Utah	21/104	20.2
Vermont	60/180	33.3
Virginia	20/140	14.3
Washington	49/147	33.3
West Virginia	21/134	15.7
Wisconsin	34/132	25.8
Wyoming	13/90	14.4
Total	**1663/7382**	**22.5%**

Source: Center for American Women and Politics, Rutgers, State University of New Jersey.

tional authority through a higher leadership position such as the House (or Assembly) or Senate leader; in these positions, women committee chairs "appear to be more comfortable developing their influence through group efforts aimed at solving a problem or achieving a desired outcome."[33]

CONCLUSION

Building on the progress that has been made in recent years, an increase in the number of women legislators at both the state and national government is inevitable. Women benefit the political process with "access to a greater diversity of ideas and experiences that fuel definition of problems and the creation of solutions."[34] In order for the number of women serving in legislatures at both the state and national level to continue to increase, strong recruitment efforts must be undertaken. Any political candidate needs an adequate amount of money as well as support from relevant interest groups and party leadership to be competitive in a campaign. Incumbent women also need to identify and mentor other women to run for similar offices.[35]

Research conducted in recent years on both Congress and state legislatures has shown that women do make a difference in policy outcomes, particularly in those policies directly affecting women. However, women have yet to have a significant impact on legislative norms and practices and how legislatures operate on a day-to-day basis. Nonetheless, women, "though few in number and relatively new to positions of institutional power, are transforming our understanding of the nature of representation and are dramatically re-shaping the agenda and representation of interests in Congress."[36] The same trend has emerged at the state level as well, as women continue to gain access to the legislative process in their quest to be equal participants in policymaking at all levels of government.

STUDY/DISCUSSION QUESTIONS

1. Why is integrative or transformational leadership more effective in legislatures, and why might women legislators benefit from this strategy?
2. Why did women gaining the right to vote in 1920 not automatically translate into more women running for and being elected to political office?
3. How does the Congressional Caucus for Women's Issues impact the legislative agenda in Congress?
4. Why are leadership positions in Congress so important? How might women impact policymaking by holding these positions?
5. Why are state legislatures such important venues for women's issues? How do state legislatures benefit women seeking a political career?

SUGGESTED READINGS

Gertzog, Irwin N. 1995. *Congressional Women: Their Recruitment, Integration, and Behavior*, 2nd ed. Westport, CT: Praeger.
Gertzog, Irwin N. 2004. *Women and Power on Capitol Hill*. Boulder, CO: Lynne Rienner.

O'Connor, Karen, ed. 2001. *Women and Congress: Running, Winning, and Ruling*. New York: Haworth Press.

Rosenthal, Cindy Simon. 1998. *When Women Lead: Integrative Leadership in State Legislatures*. New York: Oxford University Press.

Rosenthal, Cindy Simon, ed. 2002. *Women Transforming Congress*. Norman: University of Oklahoma Press.

Thomas, Sue. 1994. *How Women Legislate*. New York: Oxford University Press.

Thomas, Sue, and Clyde Wilcox, eds. 1998. *Women and Elective Office: Past, Present, & Future*. New York: Oxford University Press.

Whitney, Catherine, et al. 2000. *Nine and Counting: The Women of the Senate*. New York: William Morrow.

ONLINE RESOURCES

http://www.house.gov. Home page for the U.S. House of Representatives.

http://www.senate.gov. Home page for the U.S. Senate.

http://www.womenspolicy.org. Women's Policy, Inc., the Unique Source of Information on Women's Issues in Congress.

http://democraticleader.house.gov. Home page for House Democratic Leader Nancy Pelosi.

NOTES

1. Cindy Simon Rosenthal, *When Women Lead: Integrative Leadership in State Legislatures* (New York: Oxford University Press, 1998), 7.
2. Ibid., 162.
3. Ibid., 21–22.
4. Ibid., 160.
5. Marie C. Wilson, *Closing the Leadership Gap: Why Women Can and Must Help Run the World* (New York: Penguin Books, 2004), 4.
6. Pat Schroeder, "Running for Our Lives: Electoral Politics," in *Sisterhood Is Forever: The Women's Anthology for a New Millennium*, ed. Robin Morgan, 28–31 (New York: Washington Square Press, 2003).
7. Ibid., 33.
8. Barbara Mikulski, quoted in Catherine Whitney et al., *Nine and Counting: The Women of the Senate* (New York: William Morrow, 2000), 117–18.
9. Barbara Boxer, quoted in Whitney, *Nine and Counting*, 47–48.

10. Sue Thomas, *How Women Legislate* (New York: Oxford University Press, 1994), 153.

11. Biography of Congresswoman Loretta Sanchez, House of Representatives Web page, accessed at http://www.lorettasanchez.house.gov/display2.cfm?id=8373&type=Home.

12. "The Changing Face of Orange County," *California Journal,* State Net, June 1, 2001.

13. Emelyn Rodriguez, "A Modern-Day Helen of Troy?" *California Journal,* State Net, June 1, 2001.

14. Thomas, *How Women Legislate,* 100.

15. Susan J. Carroll, "Representing Women: Congresswomen's Perceptions of Their Representational Roles," in *Women Transforming Congress,* ed. Cindy Simon Rosenthal, 66 (Norman: University of Oklahoma Press, 2002).

16. Olympia Snowe, quoted in Whitney, *Nine and Counting,* 129–30.

17. Whitney, *Nine and Counting,* 3.

18. Cynthia A. Hall, "The Congressional Caucus for Women's Issues at 25: Challenges and Opportunities" in *The American Woman 2003–2004: Daughters of a Revolution-Young Women Today,* ed. Cynthia B. Costello, Vanessa R. Wight, and Anne J. Stone, 348 (New York: Palgrave Macmillan, 2003).

19. Chris Suellentrop, "The Leader the House Democrats Deserve," *Slate,* November 13, 2002.

20. Sheryl Gay Stolberg, "A Nation at War: The House Minority Leader; With Democrats Divided on War, Pelosi Faces Leadership Test," *The New York Times,* March 31, 2003, p. B13.

21. Rosenthal, *When Women Lead,* 161.

22. John M. Carey, Richard G. Niemi, and Lynda W. Powell, "Are Women Legislators Different?" in *Women and Elective Office: Past, Present, & Future,* ed. Sue Thomas and Clyde Wilcox, 100–101 (New York: Oxford University Press, 1998).

23. Susan J. Carroll, "Representing Women: Women State Legislators as Agents of Policy-Related Change," in *The Impact of Women in Public Office,* ed. Susan J. Carroll (Bloomington: Indiana University Press, 2001), 17–18.

24. Carey, Niemi, and Powell, "Are Women Legislators Different?" 101.

25. Sue Thomas and Susan Welch, "The Impact of Women in State Legislatures: Numerical and Organizational Strength," in Carroll, *The Impact of Women in Public Office,* 178.

26. Lynne E. Ford and Kathleen Dolan, "Women State Legislators: Three Decades of Gains in Representation and Diversity," in

Women in Politics: Outsiders or Insiders? ed. Lois Duke Whitaker, 205 (Upper Saddle River, NJ: Prentice Hall, 1999).

27. Ibid., 216.
28. Rosenthal, *When Women Lead,* 13–14.
29. Women in Elected Office 2004 Fact Sheet Summaries, Center for American Women and Politics, Rutgers, State University of New Jersey, accessed at http://www.rci.rutgers.edu/~cawp/ Facts/Officeholders/cawpfs.html.
30. Susan J. Carroll, "Women in State Government: Historical Overview and Current Trends," in *The Book of the States 2004* (Lexington, KY: Council of State Governments, 2004), accessed at http://www.rci.rutgers.edu/~cawp/Research/Reports/ BookofStates.pdf.
31. Ibid.
32. Marcia Lynn Whicker and Malcolm Jewell, "The Feminization of Leadership in State Legislatures," in Thomas and Wilcox, *Women and Elective Office,* 174.
33. Cindy Simon Rosenthal, "Getting Things Done: Women Committee Chairpersons in State Legislatures," in Thomas and Wilcox, *Women and Elective Office,* 186.
34. Thomas, *How Women Legislate,* 147.
35. Carroll, "Women in State Government."
36. Cindy Simon Rosenthal, Introduction to *Women Transforming Congress,* ed. Cindy Simon Rosenthal (Norman: University of Oklahoma Press, 2002), 11.

Women and Executive Leadership

What would it be like if women ran the world?
—Sally Helgesen
author of The Female Advantage: Women's Ways of Leadership

Will America ever elect a women president? This has become a popular question in recent years, and has been the topic of several books, academic conferences, public opinion polls, and countless lectures in women and politics courses on college campuses across the country. Yet despite all the attention to the possibility, and many assertions by experts who say "it's not a matter of if, but when," there has been no serious female presidential contender. Pat Schroeder in 1988, Elizabeth Dole in 2000, and Carol Moseley Braun in 2004 each had short-lived presidential campaigns. Each of these women share accomplished political careers—Schroeder served 24 years in the House of Representatives from Colorado; Dole, who is currently a U.S. senator from North Carolina, previously served as both secretary of transportation and secretary of labor; and Braun is a former U.S. senator from Illinois (and the first black woman to ever serve in the Senate) who also served as U.S. ambassador to New Zealand during the Clinton administration. But each also shares one other professional experience—none of these women survived the presidential campaign process long enough to have one vote cast in their favor in a presidential primary or caucus.

While women have made great strides in achieving legislative office, as discussed in the previous chapter, there still seems to be a dearth of women executive leaders in government, business, and all institutions within American society. From the top executive spot in the Oval Office, to governors' mansions and city halls, and to corporate boardrooms across the country, executive leadership positions are still dominated by men. This chapter will discuss executive political leadership and the barriers faced by women politicians in gaining access to these seats of power. First, we will look at how women in the corporate world have defined successful leadership to determine if there are any lessons to be learned for women seeking political executive positions. Then we will consider the potential of electing a woman president, as well as the impact of women in other prominent executive positions—cabinet members and other White House staff positions, first ladies, state governors, and mayors.

EXECUTIVE LEADERSHIP FROM A WOMAN'S PERSPECTIVE

The job of the American president is often compared to that of a chief executive officer of a large corporation. Unlike positions in legislatures, which by their very nature require cooperation on some level with other members in an equal position, a president or CEO has no counterpart within the organization and is ultimately responsible for making the executive decisions. Several politicians in recent years have sought either the presidency or the position of state governor based on their successful business careers as corporate executives. Former business executives often reason that if they can run a major corporation, those same skills should transfer into running a government bureaucracy. For example, in 1992, H. Ross Perot received 19 percent of the popular vote in the presidential election based on his approach for fiscal responsibility in handling the federal budget, a skill he attributed to his long career as a leader in the corporate world.

Whether or not a successful CEO could also effectively run the executive branch of the federal government remains to be seen. However, both the political and business sectors share many masculine traditions in their structure, environment, and culture. Women have also been slow to make substantial gains in each field, if for no other reason than not enough time has passed since the women's movement of the late 1960s began to break down many of the social and cultural barriers for women seeking executive positions. Women need both time and credentials to work their way up in both business and political leadership positions. Executive positions of power have always been male dominated, and as a result, gender plays an important role in determining successful leadership traits. Consequently, a woman "cannot enter a post previously held by a male and be entirely inter-changeable with him—in meaning at least."[1]

How do women business executives fare in a male-dominated arena, and are there instructive comparisons for women governors or a future woman president? In recent years, much has been written about how women's leadership styles in the business world—those based on building inclusive relationships—were better for business than the traditional, hierarchical system. Management literature has embraced the notion of women's unique leadership qualities, as well as their emotional intelligence (the ability to recognize and control one's emotions).[2] Much has also been written in recent years about how female leadership characteristics and principles—communication, personal relationships, community building, and ignoring the rigid hierarchy of most corporations—provide an important advantage to women in the corporate world.[3] However, many of these same women fear that acknowledging a difference exists between male and female leadership traits will be the same as admitting to inequality. As a result, women are often "wedged into stereotypes, often acting against female values, trying to fit the male definition of leadership."[4]

The old paradigm of leadership, defined as masculine within a hierarchical, command-and-control structure, shows an opposition to change. This style of leadership is also defined by individual (as opposed to group) efforts, with indirect communication trickling down through the organization's vertical structure.[5] However, many successful women in business have adopted a new paradigm of leadership that has moved away from this more traditional approach. Women used to attempt to succeed by trying to be more like men, including dressing like men and managing in a structured, top-down approach that limited their access to colleagues and customers—a "command-and-control style long associated with the masculine mind-set." But by the mid-to-late 1990s, successful female corporate executives, like Meg Whitman of eBay, Inc. and Marcy Carsey of Carsey-Werner Company, had developed new strategies to grow their businesses. These new paradigm leaders are "noted for their abilities to blend feminine qualities of leadership with classic male traits to run their companies successfully, and become some of the most powerful women in American business."[6]

Esther Wachs Book, author of *Why the Best Man for the Job Is a Woman*, states that these women who adopt the new paradigm of leadership succeed for three main reasons: Self-assurance compels new paradigm leaders to stay motivated and take risks; an obsession with customer service helps them anticipate market changes; and new paradigm leaders use "feminine" traits to their advantage (empathy, collaboration, cooperation—acknowledging differences between men and women and their leadership styles make more approaches available). She also identifies seven key characteristics of new paradigm leadership: selling the vision; reinventing the rules; having a laser focus to achieve; maximizing high touch in an era of high tech; turning challenge into opportunity; having an obsession with customer preferences; and having courage under fire.[7]

Like women in politics, women in business careers also face barriers in reaching the top of the corporate ladder. Childrearing and other family responsibilities top the list, as well as incorrect stereotypes that women just are not tough enough, aggressive enough, or ambitious enough to make it to the corner office. Studies have also shown that men are often reluctant to place women in positions of power over others in work settings.[8] Perhaps the most notable recent woman CEO is Carleton S. "Carly" Fiorina of Hewlett-Packard, who had a leadership style during her six years (1999–2005) at the helm of the computer giant that even other women corporate officers admit is a tough act to follow. Fiorina succeeded in gaining her position by following the more traditional male path to power through drive and ambition, not the new paradigm of leadership. But most women in business have not followed Fiorina's model. Currently, women hold only 8 percent of the top-level jobs in major U.S. companies, which suggests, "Unbridled ambition is less acceptable in women than in men."[9] However, Fiorina's public ouster from HP in early 2005 may suggest that following the new paradigm may be the better option for women in corporate America.

According to Marie Wilson, founder of the White House Project, a nonpartisan organization dedicated to placing more women in top leadership positions within government and business, "Ambition in men is an expectation and a virtue. In women, it can be a kiss of death, guaranteeing isolation, ending relationships (personal and professional), pushing entire families into therapy, and making even the most self-assured CEO wonder what she was thinking."[10] Women, more often than men, are not willing to make family sacrifices in order to climb the corporate ladder. While Wilson views women today as equal competitors with men in terms of education, experience, and skill, success is based more on how hard a person chooses to compete rather than gender discrimination, and "the folks who tend to compete the hardest are generally the stereotypically manly men." Recent studies have also suggested that women may be happier if they give up positions of power in return for more quality time in their lives for family, friends, and other nonbusiness pursuits.[11] Nonetheless, women are often conflicted about such decisions, believing that they have somehow failed other women in their profession if they choose family over career.

A WOMAN PRESIDENT

The executive branch is perhaps the most masculine of the three branches of government, due mostly to its hierarchical structure, the unity of command, and the ability for a president to act decisively when the need arises. The presidency also "operates on the great man model of leadership," which leaves women defined as the "other" in the executive branch.[12] Creating a strong image of presidential leadership in the minds of Americans is an essential aspect of political success for any politician who aspires to the Oval Office. Strong leadership has historically been defined as an attempt to exert one's will over a particular situation, a societal view that "has been conditioned by the interpretation of American history as written." This, in turn, affects how the public will view other aspiring leaders, particularly women.[13] Also not helpful to women seeking the presidency is the notion of "presidential machismo," which is the image desired by many Americans to have their president exhibit tough and aggressive behavior on the international stage. Even though the unilateral actions of a president to wage war or carry out other military actions may run "counter to aspects of democratic theory of governance," public opinion polls routinely show that Americans admire this type of behavior by presidents, forming "the basis of a cult that often elevates presidents, primarily those regarded as strong and who waged successful wars, to the status of heroes."[14]

Once in office, presidents must remember that their job, by constitutional design, is one of both shared and limited powers. A paradox exists for presidential power, in that Americans expect great things from our presidents, but "the resources at the disposal of the president are limited and the system in which a president operates can easily frustrate efforts at presidential leadership."[15] As such, presidents must maximize their opportunities to gain influence and achieve success with their policy agendas, in dealing with Congress, and certainly in the eyes of the American public in determining job approval. Other factors must also be considered if presidents are to maximize their leadership potential, including effectiveness as a public communicator, organizational capacity (staffing and leadership style within the

White House), cognitive style (intellectual curiosity coupled with either attention to detail or abstract thinking skills), and emotional intelligence.[16] If we assume that women tend to exhibit a leadership style based on cooperation, compromise, and emotional intelligence, a woman president would be no more constrained in this area than her male counterpart and might even enjoy a strategic advantage.[17]

That assumes, however, that women presidential contenders can overcome the many electoral barriers that exist. Aside from the constitutional requirements for the office of the presidency—being at least 35 years old, a 14-year U.S. resident, and a natural born citizen—no other formal criteria exist for presidential candidates. However, "a number of informal qualifications have limited the pool of potential nominees," with factors such as religion, race, and gender, making the pool of viable candidates for both president and vice president almost exclusively Protestant, white, and male.[18] John F. Kennedy, a Catholic, remains the only non-Protestant to hold the office of the presidency. Joseph Lieberman's nomination as the first Jewish vice presidential candidate in 2000, along with the intense public interest in a possible presidential run by Gen. Colin Powell in 1996, suggest that a small amount of progress has been made in how the American public views potential candidates for president and vice president. The health and age of the candidate, as well as family ties and personal relationships (particularly marital status and fidelity), are also important characteristics for candidates.[19]

The character, personality, and style of presidential candidates are crucial in how voters evaluate those seeking the White House. While party affiliation and policy preferences are still an important factor among voters, the decline of partisan loyalty and the desire for party nominees to appeal to moderate, middle-of-the-road voters during most general election campaigns in recent decades has placed more emphasis on the candidate as an individual. During the television age, political news reporting has become more cynical, sensationalized, and hypercritical, which has led to an increased focus on the "cult of personality" during presidential campaigns.[20] Although *character* may be a broadly defined term, Americans look for honesty, integrity, intelligence, strong communication skills, flexibility, compassion, open-mindedness, and a commitment to both the public good and a democratic process in their presidential candidates.[21] For women candidates, it is even more important to develop an effective communication strategy to combat negative stereotypes in the news media (as discussed in Chapter 3) by emphasizing her "perceived image and issue strengths—honesty and trustworthiness and dealing with social concerns—as well as [establishing] her credibility as a tough and decisive leader able to handle such issues as crime, foreign policy, and the economy."[22] Showing strength and experience in the foreign policy arena is even more important for women presidential candidates in the post-9/11 era.

Where, then, do Americans find presidential and vice presidential candidates? An "on-deck circle" exists of roughly 40 individuals in any given presidential election year: governors, prominent U.S. senators, a few members of the House of Representatives, and a handful of recent governors or vice presidents who have remained prominent in the news media.[23] Other keys to success in the early days of a presidential campaign include name recognition in the news media, support among party elites, access to money (either personal wealth or successful fundraising capabilities), and time to both campaign and fundraise. In recent years, holding the office of the vice presidency or being a governor of a large state has elevated the public status of several presidential hopefuls. The Washington insider versus outsider phenomenon has also emerged; four of the last five presidents were previous state governors. The image of "master politician" (political experience and substantive policy accomplishments), once necessary to run for the White House, has given way to the image of the "Washington outsider," which requires strong speaking skills, an emphasis on anti-Washington rhetoric, and broad public appeal outside the beltway.[24] This outsider strategy proved successful for Governors Jimmy Carter of Georgia, Ronald Reagan of California, Bill Clinton of Arkansas, and George W. Bush of Texas.

Given all of the requirements necessary to be a viable presidential candidate, it starts to become obvious why no woman has yet to be elected president, received her party's nomination, or why so few have even decided to run in the first place. The most glaring problem is that so few women hold the appropriate leadership positions within our government that allow them access to the on-deck circle. There are several reasons for this, including: the traditional view that men should hold public leadership roles while women should remain at home tending to domestic responsibilities and childrearing; a political system that is biased in favor of incumbents; fewer women in elected office leave inadequate numbers of role models for younger women who might aspire to political careers; women are less likely to be recruited to run for the presidency; and finally, due to the "double burden" of work and family responsibilities from which many professional women suffer, women are more likely to run for office much later in life than men.[25] In addition, recent research has shown that the candidate emergence phase of a campaign—moving from a potential to an actual candidate—represents one of the biggest hurdles for women to overcome, particularly in seeking the presidency. A gender gap seems to exist in political ambition, which is attributed to the fact that women are significantly less likely than men to receive encouragement (either from a current or former politician or from a financial supporter) to run for office or to deem themselves qualified to run for office.[26]

The possibility of a woman being selected as a Democratic or Republican running mate in the near future should not be overlooked. More than 20 years have now passed since Geraldine Ferraro's historic bid for the vice presidency as Democrat Walter Mondale's running mate in 1984, and public anticipation for the second female running mate has remained high in recent years. While the vice presidential selection process is based on how best to help the party's nominee win the White House, the vice presidency is also a popular route to the Oval Office. Of 42 vice presidents in our nation's history, 14 have become president—5 were elected, 8 succeeded to the office upon the death of the president, and Gerald Ford became president following Richard Nixon's resignation in 1974. Balancing the ticket is usually a goal of the nominee and his party, and is usually done in terms of ideology, geography, experience, and insider versus outsider status (a vice president who is a Washington insider may later help with congressional relationships for an outsider president). Healing a breach within the party and whether or not the running mate hails from an electorally rich state may also be considerations. Today's vice presidential nominees "must possess some desirable qualities the presidential nominee lacks and must be acceptable to the presidential nominee . . . [although there is] little evidence to suggest that vice presidents add greatly to or detract severely from the popularity of presidential candidates with the voters."[27]

Despite the many barriers for a woman to be elected president, public opinion suggests continued support for electing a woman president, at least in theory. A February 2005 poll by the Siena College Research Institute found that 6 out of 10 voters are ready for a woman president and that 81 percent of those surveyed would vote for a woman president. Potential candidates for 2008 that topped the survey included New York Senator Hillary Rodham Clinton for the Democrats and Secretary of State Condoleezza Rice and North Carolina Senator Elizabeth Dole for the Republicans.[28] These types of poll results have been common in recent years. A Gallup poll in May 2003 found that 87 percent of Americans are willing to vote for a qualified woman for president. Similarly, a Roper poll in February 2003 found that 76 percent of

WOMEN AND THE RACE FOR THE WHITE HOUSE:

The Contenders

The first female candidate for the presidency dates back to 1872, when Victoria Woodhull, a stockbroker, publisher, and protégé of Cornelius Vanderbilt, ran for president on the Equal Rights Party ticket. She was followed by Belva Lockwood, the first woman admitted to practice law before the U.S. Supreme Court and an active participant in the women's suffrage movement, who ran for president on the same party ticket in 1884 and 1888. Eight decades would pass before the next woman would officially seek the presidency. Senator Margaret Chase Smith, a Maine Republican, dropped out of the race after placing fifth in the New Hampshire primary. Smith, who made history by becoming the first woman to serve in both houses of Congress (elected to the House of Representatives in 1940 to replace her dying husband and to the Senate in 1948), was also nominated for the presidency by Vermont Senator George Aiken at the Republican national convention in 1964.

Shirley Chisholm, the first black woman to serve in Congress (a Democrat in the House of Representatives from New York), ran for president in 1972. In doing so, Chisholm stunned friends and colleagues with her decision, yet used her candidacy to raise awareness of issues such as education and other social programs within the Democratic presidential primary. Even though Chisholm's name was placed on the ballot in 12 primary states, she never received more than 7 percent of the vote in any of the primary contests.[29]

Since then, no woman in either major political party has sustained a presidential campaign long enough to have a vote cast

"influential Americans" think that a woman will be elected president within the next 20 years. Other polls also suggest a "desire for women's leadership at the pinnacle of government."[30] However, still other surveys have shown a decrease in support for electing a woman president in the aftermath of the 9/11 terrorist attacks. Respondents showed a preference for men's leadership traits and characteristics over those of women, and a belief that men are more competent and superior to handling issues related to national security and terrorism in the post-9/11 in her favor in the earliest contests—the Iowa Caucus and the New Hampshire Primary. Pat Schroeder seriously considered a run for the presidency in 1988 after Democratic frontrunner Gary Hart dropped out of the race in the spring of 1987. Her campaign, however, never made it out of the exploratory mode and had officially ended by September 1987. Elizabeth Dole had a much stronger campaign organization going into the 2000 Republican primaries, yet when money and positive news coverage both became elusive in the fall of 1999, she too withdrew from the presidential race.

Unlike Schroeder and Dole, who both fared well enough in early public opinion polls to give their campaigns temporary credibility, Carol Moseley Braun's campaign for the 2004 Democratic presidential nomination was a long shot from the outset. Nonetheless, while she dropped out of the race in January 2004, prior to the Iowa Caucus, Moseley Braun made it onto a total of 20 primary ballots, more than any other woman, Democrat or Republican, had ever achieved. She also performed well in several televised debates as the only woman in a field of mostly white men, and was credited with bringing a unique voice to the political discussion in the early days of the 2004 presidential race. She also had a major player within the women's rights movement as her campaign manager—Patricia Ireland, prominent feminist author and former president of the National Organization for Women. Moseley Braun's favorite line while out on the campaign trail told voters why they should take her candidacy seriously: "The final reason to vote for me is that I'm the clearest alternative to George Bush. I don't look like him. I don't talk like him. I don't think like him. And I certainly don't act like him."[31]

world.[32] This suggests that there may be some disconnect between the results of some polls that provide an optimistic outlook for women presidential candidates and the reality of how voters will actually respond in the current political environment.

The gender, education, and political ideology of the respondents in polls about electing a woman president seem to be the most prominent factors that shape public opinion, followed by age, race, and party identification.[33] Yet, potential women presidential and vice presidential candidates are not portrayed as authoritative in the press. Much like Ferraro in 1984, Elizabeth Dole's coverage in 1999 "was covered more as a novelty than a serious candidate," what the White House Project referred to as the "hair, hemlines, and husbands" approach to coverage.[34] Other studies in recent years have also showed this trend, making gender a significant, and not always positive, label in news media coverage for women candidates.[35]

WOMEN IN THE EXECUTIVE BRANCH

While no woman has yet served as president or vice president, women have taken an increasingly prominent role in other positions throughout the executive branch. Beginning in the 1960s and continuing through the 1970s, the link between the presidency and women—both in terms of appointments within the executive branch and in terms of policies relevant to women—became much stronger. During the 1980s, in spite of Ronald Reagan's appointment of the first woman to the U.S. Supreme Court, the number of overall appointments of women to positions within the administration declined. With George H. W. Bush's election in 1988, the numbers again increased, as well as the attention paid to women's issues.[36] The two most recent presidents, Bill Clinton and George W. Bush, have appointed women to executive posts in record numbers, in part as recognition for the political importance of women voters and interest groups devoted to women's issues. Three avenues of influence for women within both the White House and the federal bureaucracy include presidential appointments to cabinet and other cabinet-level positions, posts within the White House as presidential advisors, and the unofficial yet sometimes powerful role of the first lady.

The President's Cabinet

As we discussed in Chapter 1, since the presidential cabinet was established in 1789, women have held only 35 cabinet or cabinet-level positions. Frances Perkins became the first woman to ever serve in the cabinet when Franklin D. Roosevelt appointed her as secretary of labor. Madeleine Albright, who served as secretary of state during Bill Clinton's administration (1996–2001), became the highest-ranking woman ever to serve in the cabinet. The rank of cabinet offices is based on presidential succession, as well as the four "inner" cabinet positions that have been designated as such by presidency scholars in recent years due to the influence of the positions in national policymaking. The inner cabinets include the Departments of State, Justice, Defense, and Treasury. According to the Presidential Succession Act of 1947, cabinet members follow the vice president, Speaker of the House of Representatives, and the president pro tempore of the Senate based on the date their offices were established. The first four cabinet members in line for succession include, in order: secretary of state, secretary of treasury, secretary of defense, and the attorney general. However, Albright could not have served as president due to the constitutional requirement that presidents must be natural born citizens, since she was born in Czechoslovakia.

During the mid-twentieth century, women cabinet appointments were usually viewed as tokenism within an administration. By the 1990s, however, the political climate had changed and public expectations had shifted as women cabinet appointments began to be seen as a more routine presidential practice. At the start of his administration in 2001, George W. Bush appointed three women to his cabinet— Elaine Chao (Labor), Gale Norton (Interior), and Ann Veneman (Agriculture)—as well as appointing Christine Todd Whitman to the cabinet-level position as head of the Environmental Protection Agency. Bush sought to follow the example set by his predecessor, Bill Clinton, in appointing a cabinet that looked like America in terms of gender and ethnic diversity. A total of five women had served in cabinet positions during Clinton's two terms in office. And, Bush included two women appointees to his second-term cabinet, including Condoleezza Rice's move from national security advisor to secretary of state (see Table 6.1).

A president's nomination to a cabinet post is a signal of representation—the nominee for a particular cabinet position reflects the president's agenda in that particular area of policy. As such, the cabinet secretary represents the president's policy agenda to relevant constituents (voters, interest groups, Congress, state and local governments). While many of the women who have served in the cabinet have done so in positions of influence over "women's issues," particularly in the departments of Health and Human Services and Labor, appointments in recent years suggest that women are now being considered for a wider variety of posts within an administration. However, based on news media coverage and treatment during the confirmation process in the Senate, many of these women cabinet members are still viewed as token appointments within the administration. One recent study suggests "women have yet to be perceived as full participants in the cabinet, either as office holders or as constituents."[37]

TABLE 6.1 Women in the Cabinet—1933 to Present

State
Madeleine Albright, 1996–2001 (Clinton)
Condoleezza Rice, 2005–Present (Bush)

Treasury
None

Defense
None

Justice
Janet Reno, 1993–2001 (Clinton)

Interior
Gale Norton, 2001–Present (Bush)

Agriculture
Ann Veneman, 2001–2005 (Bush)

Commerce
Juanita Kreps, 1977–1979 (Carter)
Barbara Franklin, 1992–1993 (Bush)

Labor
Frances Perkins, 1933–1945 (Roosevelt)
Ann McLaughlin, 1987–1989 (Reagan)
Elizabeth Dole, 1989–1991 (Bush)
Lynn Martin, 1991–1993 (Bush)
Alexis Herman, 1997–2001 (Clinton)
Elaine Chao, 2001–Present (Bush)

Health and Human Services (formerly Health, Education and Welfare)
Oveta Culp Hobby, 1953–1955 (Eisenhower)
Patricia Roberts Harris, 1979–1981 (Carter)
Margaret Heckler, 1983–1985 (Reagan)
Donna Shalala, 1993–2001 (Clinton)

Housing and Urban Development
Carla Anderson Hills, 1975–1977 (Ford)
Patricia Roberts Harris, 1977–1979 (Carter)

Transportation
Elizabeth Dole, 1983–1987 (Reagan)

Energy
Hazel O'Leary, 1993–1997 (Clinton)

Education
Shirley Mount Hufstedler, 1979–1981 (Carter)
Margaret Spellings, 2005–Present (Bush)

Veterans Affairs
None

Homeland Security
None

White House Advisors

The size of the White House staff has grown dramatically during the past century. With the creation of the Executive Office of the President in 1937, a formal staff put into place during Franklin Roosevelt's second term in office to help with the implementation of New Deal policies, the president's inner circle of advisors has grown in both numbers and influence. With the increase in the role of the federal government in policymaking in the post-New Deal era, White House staffers now perform "integral and influential roles in both presidential policymaking and politics."[38] Women have made substantial gains in obtaining White House staff positions in recent years, particularly during the administrations of Bill Clinton and George W. Bush. However, a glass ceiling still seems to exist in allowing women access to the president's inner circle of closest advisors. Even when women are appointed to White House staff positions, their positions tend to be more political than related to the policymaking process within the White House.[39]

As Bush's national security advisor during his first term, and moving into the job of secretary of state in his second term, Condoleezza Rice is a prominent exception to that rule. Rice played an integral role in drafting the Bush administration's foreign policy strategy in the war on terrorism as well as the invasion of Iraq following the terrorist attacks on September 11, 2001. During the first Bush term, Rice was "by far the closest [advisor] to Bush," and was of "critical importance" in helping Bush reach foreign policy decisions, particularly when other senior advisors were at odds over proposed courses of action. As a result, Rice "operated at the interface between the President and his political advisors, on the one hand, and his foreign policy team, on the other."[40] However, despite Rice's prominent White House role, along with Communications Director Karen Hughes, who represented one of the other most powerful and influential advisors in the early years of the Bush administration, no woman has yet served as a chief of staff and only a handful of women have ever earned the title, as Hughes did, "special assistant to the president."

Dee Dee Myers, who served as Clinton's first press secretary (and the first woman to ever hold the job), was certainly a visible member of the Clinton team through daily press briefings. However, she had difficulty performing her duties as she was routinely excluded from the inner-circle access to information found among Clinton's closest advisors. Situational and structural barriers also exist for women seeking top staff positions within the White House.

Not only do women with family responsibilities realize many political career opportunities somewhat later in life than their male counterparts, much of the White House staff comes from the president's campaign staff, where women rarely play a major role.[41] Hughes, who was a close advisor to Bush in her capacity as communications director in both his 2000 campaign and in the first two years of his administration, opted to leave her position to return to her home state of Texas during her son's high school years. (She did, however, continue to play an advisory role from afar during the president's reelection campaign during 2004.)[42]

The First Lady

The role of the first lady, as wife of the president, is a private one with public duties. There is no constitutional mandate or description for the job, yet many first ladies have served their husbands "as policy advisers and political assistants—some privately, some more publicly."[43] The public role for first ladies has mostly been a social one, yet several first ladies during the twentieth century provide distinct examples of the power and influence that can come with the position. Each woman has been allowed to determine her own role within her husband's administration. Some, like Mamie Eisenhower, Ladybird Johnson, Barbara Bush, and Laura Bush, have opted for a more traditional, nonpublic role in their husband's White House. Others, like Edith Wilson, Eleanor Roosevelt, Rosalyn Carter, and Hillary Rodham Clinton, opted for active involvement in policy decisions and publicly acknowledged their political role within the administration.

While each first lady shapes her own role within the White House, the fundamental duties of the modern first lady include some or all of the following: wife and mother; public figure and celebrity; nation's social hostess; symbol of the American woman; White House manager and preservationist; campaigner; social advocate and champion of social causes; presidential spokesperson; presidential and political party booster; diplomat; and political and presidential partner.[44] The Office of the First Lady has become, in recent years, part of the official organizational structure of the Office of the President. One of the main responsibilities of the first lady's staff is in the day-to-day dealings with the news media. In addition to a press secretary, most first ladies have also employed a chief of staff, a social secretary, a projects director (for causes that a first lady may adopt, like Barbara Bush's commitment to literacy), and several other special assistants. Since the 1970s, first ladies have employed anywhere between 12 to 28 full-time employees for their staffs.[45]

Perhaps no first lady has so stretched the boundaries of what the nation expects from the president's wife more than did Hillary Rodham Clinton, who made history in 2000 when she won a U.S. Senate seat in New York. She writes in her memoirs of her White House years that first ladies, due to being married to the man who becomes president, have a "position" but not a real "job." "There is no training manual for First Ladies. . . . Like all First Ladies before me, I had to decide what I wanted to do with the opportunities and responsibilities I had inherited."[46] As a successful attorney with her own political ambitions, as well as having an active role in policy decisions, Clinton proved to be both an asset and liability during her husband's presidential campaigns and his two terms in office. From the early days of Clinton's first presidential campaign, when he told voters that they would get "two for the price of one" if he were elected, "Hillary bashing" in the press became routine as many political pundits questioned whether she planned to act as a co-president.[47] Her choice of an office within the West Wing of the White House among the president's top advisors, the only first lady to have an office outside the East Wing, signaled from the start her intention to be a full partner in the presidency with her husband.

Soon after her husband's inauguration, Clinton accepted a formal position within the White House as chair of the President's Task Force on National Health Reform. Two other first ladies had also held formal positions, including Eleanor Roosevelt as the assistant director for the Office of Civilian Defense from September 1941 to February 1942, and Rosalyn Carter as honorary chair of the President's Commission on Mental Health from February 1977 to April 1978. But unlike her two predecessors, Clinton's appointment to oversee the creation of the task force gave tremendous political influence and formal power over a major area of domestic policy to a first lady. Bill Clinton had made reforming the nation's health care system a major issue during his campaign, and he touted his wife's experience as having chaired various policy-related committees while he was governor of Arkansas in why she was the best possible person for the job. In spite of Clinton's previous political experience, the challenge of reforming the nation's health care proved to be too much for the first lady. While she was given high praise for both the task force report and her testimony before Congress, health care reform was considered "dead on arrival" on Capitol

Hill by the end of the congressional session in 1994. As a result, Clinton kept a much lower public profile in terms of policy advice for her husband, and embraced more traditional activities for a first lady, like working on social programs. Not until 2000, when she made history by running for the U.S. Senate, did Clinton "again lay claim to formal political power."[48]

GOVERNORS AND OTHER STATEWIDE POSITIONS

State governors have served an important political function throughout the history of the United States. Not only are governors key players in the implementation of public policy at the state level, but they also serve as an important liaison in the creation of federal policy that impacts state funding of programs. This role has become crucial in the past two decades, as Congress has given more control and responsibility to states in the implementation of major federal programs like welfare. As a result, governors perhaps hold more power and influence now than ever before, not only in overseeing their state budgets and bureaucracies but in policymaking within Washington, DC, as well. Like the presidency, governorships have also been traditionally male-dominated bastions of power, and four of the last five men elected president were state governors (Carter, Reagan, Clinton, and Bush).

Women have historically not had an easy time winning their state's highest political office, and many women gubernatorial candidates have been harmed by negative attitudes and stereotypes that suggest a woman cannot succeed in such a powerful executive position. With so few women having served as state governors, research to determine leadership styles of women in this position or trends in their impact on policymaking has yet to provide definitive answers. However, the face of the state governor is finally starting to change.[49] Recent trends have shown that most women running for governor have previous political experience at either the local or state level, and that women candidates are most successful when running in open-seat elections (as opposed to an attempt to unseat an incumbent).[50] Another recent study also considered the impact of gender on gubernatorial personality and how governors exert political power. Female governors were more likely than male governors to express a more "feminine" approach to their public duties (empowering others in the political process as opposed to wielding power over others), yet they were also just as likely to take a more "masculine, power over" approach when necessary to adapt to the traditionally male-dominated political environment.[51]

As of 2005, a total of 8 women were serving as state governors, which is the most women who have ever served in this position simultaneously. A total of 28 women have served as governor in 21 states (18 Democrats and 10 Republicans). Of those, 18 were elected in their own right, 3 replaced their husbands, and 7 became governor by constitutional succession. Arizona is the only state where a woman governor has ever been succeeded by another woman, and boasts the largest number—3—of women to hold the position. Rose Mofford, a Democrat, was elected secretary of state in 1986, and succeeded to governor in 1988 after the impeachment and conviction of Governor Evan Mecham. Mofford served as governor until 1991. Jane Dee Hull, a Republican, also began her ascent to governor as the Arizona secretary of state, and succeeded to governor in 1997 upon the resignation of Fife Symington, who had been convicted of fraud. Hull was elected to a full term in 1998, when Arizona became the only state to have an all-female line of succession with women holding the offices of governor, secretary of state (Betsey Bayless), attorney general (Janet Napolitano), treasurer (Carol Springer), and superintendent of public instruction (Lisa Graham Keegan). Janet Napolitano, a Democrat who made Senator John Kerry's short list for a running mate in the 2004 presidential contest, succeeded Hull as governor in 2003.[52]

While the governor's office of large states is one of the most likely stepping-stones to the White House, only one of the six largest electoral states (California, New York, Texas, Florida, Illinois, and Pennsylvania) has ever elected a woman as governor—Democrat Ann Richards served one term as Texas governor, elected in 1990 but defeated by George W. Bush in her reelection effort in 1994. (Richards is the second woman governor in Texas; Miriam Amanda "Ma" Ferguson, a Democrat, served as governor from 1925 to 1927 and 1933 to 1935, replacing her husband, who was impeached). Nellie Tayloe Ross, a Wyoming Democrat, became the nation's first woman governor in 1925 when she replaced her husband after he died in office. Ross served for two years, and later became vice chair of the Democratic National Committee and director of the U.S. Mint. At the 1928 Democratic National Convention, she received 31 votes on the first ballot for vice president. Ella Grasso, a Democrat from Connecticut who served from 1975 to 1980, was the first woman elected as governor in her own right. Republicans would not elect their first woman governor until 1986 with the election of Kay A. Orr of Nebraska.

Other statewide positions serve as important political stepping-stones for women who seek the office of governor, or an ever higher elected political position. As of 2005, 16 women serve as state lieutenant governor, 12 as secretary of state, 4 as attorney general, 10 as state treasurer, 7 as state auditor, and 3 as state controller. Ten states have a woman as their chief education official, and 11 women serve in other statewide offices. Nationwide, women hold 79 of the 315 statewide elective positions (25.1 percent; 41 Republican, 35 Democrat, and 3 nonpartisan). Every state except Maine (which elects only the governor) and West Virginia has elected at least one woman to statewide office.

MAYORS

Historically, women have played a much larger role in the political process at the local level. Many women who would go on to have successful political careers at a much higher level began their careers in elected positions at the city level. In 1887, Susanna Salter was elected mayor of Argonia, Kansas, to become the nation's first woman mayor. Bertha K. Landes, the Republican city council president at the time, became acting mayor of Seattle in 1924, the first woman to lead a major American city. Two years later she was elected mayor in her own right in a campaign run by women, but lost in her bid for a second full term. As of May 2005, a total of 180 women were serving as mayors of cities with a population of 30,000 or more. Of these, the woman who heads the largest city within that group is Laura Miller of Dallas, which has a population of more than 1.18 million. (Other women mayors of major metropolitan cities include Mayor Jane Campbell of Cleveland, Ohio, and Mayor Shirley Franklin of Atlanta, Georgia—see Table 6.2.).

Miller was elected mayor in 2002 after serving for three-and-a-half years on the city council. Miller's agenda while mayor has been diverse, showing support for business interests with a revitalization project in downtown Dallas and support for a new convention center, while also looking out for the social needs of citizens with initiatives for affordable housing and a new intake center for the city's homeless population. Prior to entering Dallas city politics, Miller was a newspaper reporter for several papers, including the *Dallas Morning News*, *The New York Daily News*, the *Miami Herald*, and the alternative newspaper the *Dallas Observer*. While working as a journalist, she would write columns in which she routinely took city officials to task for their incompetence and malfeasance. To date, Miller has earned a

TABLE 6.2 Twenty Largest U.S. Cities with Women Mayors

Mayor	City/State	City Population
Laura Miller	Dallas, TX	1,188,580
Jane Campbell	Cleveland, OH	478,403
Beverly O'Neill	Long Beach, CA	471,000
Kay Barnes	Kansas City, MO	441,545
Meyera E. Oberndorf	Virginia Beach, VA	425,257
Shirley Franklin	Atlanta, GA	416,474
Heather Fargo	Sacramento, CA	407,018
Pam Iorio	Tampa, FL	303,447
Teresa Isaac	Lexington, KY	260,512
Coleen Seng	Lincoln, NE	225,581
Pat Evans	Plano, TX	222,030
Elaine M. Scruggs	Glendale, AZ	218,812
Mary Manross	Scottsdale, AZ	202,705
Jill Hardy	Huntington Beach, CA	189,594
Judith Valles	San Bernardino, CA	185,401
Elizabeth G. Flores	Laredo, TX	176,576
Rhine L. McLin	Dayton, OH	166,179
Loretta Spencer	Huntsville, AL	158,216
Anna M. Caballero	Salinas, CA	151,060
Jane Bender	Santa Rosa, CA	147,595

Source: Center for American Women and Politics, Rutgers, State University of New Jersey.

reputation as a pragmatic yet sometimes abrasive politician. Although not the first woman mayor of Dallas, whose leadership had always come from the male-dominated worlds of oil, real estate, and other corporate sectors, Miller has governed with a style of independent leadership by challenging the status quo.[53] By doing so, she has strengthened the power of the mayor's office, which had often been viewed as a ceremonial position among the Dallas elite.

Recent studies on the impact of women mayors suggests that there may be more gendered expectations for a woman to lead differently than there are measurable gendered differences. Given the nature of local politics, and the types of social issues that mayors must deal with, policy issues at the city level could be more easily labeled "feminine" as opposed to "masculine." For example, education and social welfare programs are critical issues for cities, and often benefit from leadership qualities associated with femininity and nurturing. This view of leadership at the city level calls into question the notion of masculine executive leadership.[54] However, like research on women in higher executive political positions, future research as more women enter these positions will provide a clearer picture of the impact that women may bring to the political process as executive leaders.

CONCLUSION

While women have certainly made progress during the past decade in breaking down more barriers to executive positions of political power, reaching gender parity within these leadership positions is still many years away. However, having women in such integral national positions such as secretary of state (Madeleine Albright and Condoleezza Rice), attorney general (Janet Reno), and national security advisor (Condoleezza Rice) can go a long way in changing social and cultural attitudes toward women in positions of power within our government. The election of more women state governors is also crucial to increase the number of women in the on-deck circle for potential presidential or vice presidential candidates in future campaigns. Recent studies have begun to focus more intently on the consequences of masculinism dominating executive politics. These consequences include a loss of talent by limiting the candidate pool to men only; a constrained worldview with a limited set of experiences for solving problems; and a loss of legitimacy for the government itself with women voters. An absence of women in executive political positions also perpetuates the myth that this is a male-only arena.[55]

Despite all the progress for women seeking political careers, the United States still lags behind several other countries, some with much more conservative political cultures, in terms of electing women to executive leadership positions. While no other national system of government matches the constitutional uniqueness found within the American system of government, other countries have nonetheless selected women as their chief executives (including Great Britain, Ireland, the Philippines, Israel, Argentina, Iceland, Pakistan, Nicaragua, and Sri Lanka). Many of these women were elected prime minister through a parliamentary system of government, which means that they did not have to win election through the support of a national constituency of voters. Instead, they needed to win only their local legislative seat, and then gained the support of their party colleagues within parliament to be elevated to prime minister. However, different societal expectations are beginning to emerge for women in American politics, and the recent trend of women entering more executive political positions, whether through election or appointment, suggests that America may be moving closer to its first woman president.

STUDY/DISCUSSION QUESTIONS

1. How do executive political positions differ from legislative positions? Why is the executive branch known as a male-dominated institution?
2. What obstacles do women face in pursuing executive leadership positions, both in the corporate world and in national and state politics?
3. When will America elect its first woman president? What changes might a woman bring to the executive branch and White House?
4. How important are cabinet members and presidential advisors in the day-to-day operation of the White House? How have women made a difference in these positions in recent years?
5. How influential should a first lady be in her husband's administration? What will be the role of the eventual "first husband"?
6. Why have so few women ever served as state governors? What impact do women governors have on the political process?
7. Why does the job of a mayor call into question the notion of masculine executive leadership?

SUGGESTED READINGS

Borrelli, MaryAnne. 2002. *The President's Cabinet: Gender, Power, and Representation.* Boulder, CO: Lynne Rienner.

Borrelli, MaryAnne, and Janet M. Martin, eds. 1997. *The Other Elites: Women, Politics, and Power in the Executive Branch.* Boulder, CO: Lynne Rienner.

Clift, Eleanor, and Tom Brazaitis. 2000. *Madam President: Shattering the Last Glass Ceiling.* New York: Scribner's Sons.

Clinton, Hillary Rodham. 2003. Living History. New York: Simon & Schuster.

Martin, Janet M. 2003. *The Presidency and Women: Promise, Performance & Illusion.* College Station: Texas A&M University Press.

Watson, Robert P. 2000. *The Presidents' Wives: Reassessing the Office of First Lady.* Boulder, CO: Lynne Rienner.

Watson, Robert P., and Ann Gordon, eds. 2003. *Anticipating Madam President.* Boulder, CO: Lynne Rienner.

ONLINE RESOURCES

http://www.thewhitehouseproject.org. The White House Project.
http://www.americanwomenpresidents.org. American Women Presidents.

http://www.womensleadership.com/. Institute for Women's
    Leadership.
http://iwl.rutgers.edu/. The Institute for Women's Leadership at
    Rutgers University.
http://www.advancingwomen.com. Advancing Women.
http://www.whitehouse.gov/history/firstladies. The First Ladies
    Gallery.

NOTES

1. Georgia Duerst-Lahti, "Reconceiving Theories of Power: Conse-
   quences of Masculinism in the Executive Branch," in *The Other
   Elites: Women, Politics, and Power in the Executive Branch,* ed.
   MaryAnne Borrelli and Janet M. Martin, 12 (Boulder, CO:
   Lynne Rienner, 1997).
2. Marie C. Wilson, *Closing the Leadership Gap: Why Women Can and
   Must Help Run the World* (New York: Penguin Books, 2004), 8.
3. For example, see Sally Helgesen, *The Female Advantage: Women's
   Ways of Leadership* (New York: Doubleday, 1990); and Candy
   Deemer and Nancy Fredericks, *Dancing on the Glass Ceiling*
   (Chicago: Contemporary Books, 2003).
4. Helgesen, *The Female Advantage,* 3.
5. Esther Wachs Book, *Why the Best Man for the Job Is a Woman: The
   Unique Female Qualities of Leadership* (New York: HarperCollins,
   2000), 15–16.
6. Ibid., 2–5.
7. Ibid., 8–14.
8. Alice H. Eagly and Mary C. Johannesen-Schmidt, "The Leadership Styles of Women and Men," *Journal of Social Sciences* 57,
   no. 4 (2001): 795.
9. Patricia Sellers, "Most Powerful Women in Business: Power—
   Do Women Really Want It?" *Fortune,* September 29, 2003.
10. Wilson, *Closing the Leadership Gap,* 53.
11. Linda Tischler, "Where Are the Women?" *Fast Company* (Febru-
    ary 2004): 52.
12. Duerst-Lahti, "Reconceiving Theories of Power," 18.
13. M. Margaret Conway, Gertrude A. Steuernagel, and Davis W.
    Ahern, *Women and Political Participation: Cultural Change in the
    Political Arena* (Washington, DC: Congressional Quarterly Press,
    1997), 100.
14. Alexander DeConde, *Presidential Machismo: Executive Authority,
    Military Intervention, and Foreign Relations* (Boston: Northeastern
    University Press, 2000), 5.

15. Thomas E. Cronin and Michael A. Genouese, *The Paradoxes of the American Presidency* (New York: Oxford University Press, 1998), 32–37.
16. Fred I. Greenstein, "George W. Bush and the Ghosts of Presidents Past," *PS: Political Science and Politics* XXXIV, no, 1 (March 2001): 77–80.
17. Lori Cox Han, "Presidential Leadership: Governance from a Woman's Perspective," in *Anticipating Madam President*, ed. Robert P. Watson and Ann Gordon, 171 (Boulder, CO: Lynne Rienner, 2003).
18. Stephen J. Wayne, *The Road to the White House 2000: The Politics of Presidential Elections, Post-election Edition* (New York: Bedford/St. Martin's Press, 2001), 185.
19. Ibid., 187–89.
20. For a discussion on this trend in news coverage, see Thomas E. Patterson, *Out of Order* (New York: Vintage Books, 1994); and Larry J. Sabato, *Feeding Frenzy: Attack Journalism and American Politics* (Baltimore: Lanahan, 2000).
21. Cronin and Genovese, *The Paradoxes of the American Presidency*, 32–37.
22. Dianne Bystrom, "On the Way to the White House: Communication Strategies for Women Candidates," in Watson and Gordon, *Anticipating Madam President*, 104.
23. Ibid., 31.
24. Richard W. Waterman, Robert Wright, and Gilbert St. Clair, *The Image-Is-Everything Presidency: Dilemmas in American Leadership* (Boulder, CO: Westview Press, 1999), 39–42.
25. Erika Falk and Kathleen Hall Jamieson, "Changing the Climate of Expectations," in Watson and Gordon, *Anticipating Madam President*, 45–47.
26. Richard L. Fox and Jennifer L. Lawless, "Entering the Arena? Gender and the Decision to Run for Office," *American Journal of Political Science* 48, no. 2 (April 2004): 264–80.
27. Nelson W. Polsby and Aaron Wildavsky, *Presidential Elections: Strategies and Structures of American Politics*, 10th ed. (New York: Chatham House, 2000), 143–45.
28. "Poll: Majority Ready for Woman President," *USA Today*, February 22, 2005.
29. Eleanor Clift and Tom Brazaitis, *Madam President: Shattering the Last Glass Ceiling* (New York: Scribner's Sons, (2000), 28.
30. Wilson, *Closing the Leadership Gap*, 17.
31. Alexandra Marks, "The Quest of Carol Moseley Braun," *The Christian Science Monitor*, November 19, 2003.

32. Jennifer L. Lawless, "Women, War, and Winning Elections: Gender Stereotyping in the Post-September 11th Era," *Political Research Quarterly* 53, no. 3 (September 2004): 479–90.

33. Kate Kenski and Erika Falk, "Of What Is This Glass Ceiling Made? A Study of Attitudes About Women and the Oval Office," *Women & Politics* 26, no. 2 (2004): 57–80.

34. Wilson, 36.

35. Diane J. Heith, "The Lipstick Watch: Media Coverage, Gender, and Presidential Campaigns," in Watson and Gordon, *Anticipating Madam President*, 123–25.

36. Janet M. Martin, *The Presidency and Women: Promise, Performance & Illusion* (College Station: Texas A&M University Press, 2003), 6–7.

37. MaryAnne Borrelli, *The President's Cabinet: Gender, Power, and Representation* (Boulder, CO: Lynne Rienner, 2002), 214.

38. Kathryn Dunn Tenpas, "Women on the White House Staff: A Longitudinal Analysis, 1939–1994," in Borrelli and Martin, *The Other Elites*, 91.

39. Ibid., 92–93.

40. James Mann, *Rise of the Vulcans: The History of Bush's War Cabinet* (New York: Viking Press, 2004), 315.

41. Ibid., 99–101.

42. Anne Marie O'Connor, "Hughes Answers the Call; Advisor Who Resigned to Spend More Time with Her Family Is Rejoining the Bush Team," *Los Angeles Times*, April 12, 2004, p. E1.

43. Barbara C. Burrell, "The Office of the First Lady and Public Policy making," in Borrelli and Martin, *The Other Elites*, 169.

44. Robert P. Watson, *The Presidents' Wives: Reassessing the Office of First Lady* (Boulder, CO: Lynne Rienner, 2000), 72.

45. Ibid., 112–13.

46. Hillary Rodham Clinton, *Living History* (New York: Simon & Schuster, 2003), 119.

47. Betty Houchin Winfield, "The First Lady, Political Power, and the Media: Who Elected Her Anyway?" in *Women, Media, and Politics*, ed. Pippa Norris (New York: Oxford University Press, 1997), 166–79.

48. MaryAnne Borrelli, "The First Lady as Formal Advisor to the President: When East (Wing) Meets West (Wing)," *Women & Politics* 24, no. 1 (2002): 25–45.

49. Brenda DeVore Marshall and Molly A. Mayhead, "The Changing Face of the Governorship," in *Navigating Boundaries: The Rhetoric of Women Governors*, ed. Brenda DeVore Marshall and Molly A. Mayhead (Westport, CT: Praeger, 2000), 14.

50. Sara J. Wier, "The Feminist Face of State Executive Leadership: Women as Governors," in *Women in Politics: Outsiders or Insiders,* ed. Lois Duke Whitaker (Upper Saddle River, NJ: Prentice Hall, 1999), 254.

51. Jay Barth and Margaret R. Ferguson, "Gender and Gubernatorial Personality," *Women & Politics* 24, no. 1 (2002): 63–82.

52. Fact Sheet, *Women Governors 1925–2004,* Center for American Women and Politics, February 2004, accessed at http://www.rci.rutgers.edu/~cawp/Facts/Officeholders/stwide.pdf.

53. John Nichols, "From Muckraker to Mayor," *The Nation,* February 18, 2002.

54. Sue Tolleson-Rinehart, "Do Women Leaders Make a Difference?" in *The Impact of Women in Public Office,* ed. Susan J. Carroll (Bloomington: Indiana University Press, 2001), 149–65.

55. Duerst-Lahti, "Reconceiving Theories of Power," 25.

CHAPTER 7

Women in the Judiciary

I have been called the most powerful woman in the United States.

—Sandra Day O'Connor
Associate Justice of the U.S. Supreme Court

Who is the most powerful woman in the United States? Several women in both the political and corporate worlds would probably top the list, but U.S. Supreme Court Associate Justice Sandra Day O'Connor would certainly be among them. She herself has stated that many people believe that as the first woman appointed to the nation's highest court, she wields tremendous power within the governing process. During the 1980 presidential campaign, Ronald Reagan promised that if he were elected, he would nominate the first woman to the U.S. Supreme Court. His first year in office, he made good on that promise by nominating O'Connor, who at the time was a member of the Arizona State Court of Appeals. Despite having graduated third in her class at Stanford Law School, perennially one of the top law schools in the nation, in 1952 (Chief Justice William Rehnquist graduated first in the same class), O'Connor had experienced a difficult time finding work as an attorney in private practice. Instead, she embarked on a career of mostly public positions, including assistant state attorney general and a state senator in Arizona.

Upon O'Connor's historic appointment to the Supreme Court, Reagan was criticized from both liberals and conservatives for his choice. Liberals were happy to see the first woman join the high court, but feared that her positions, particularly on women's issues, would be too conservative. Conservatives, on the other hand, feared that she lacked adequate federal judicial experience and knowledge of the U.S. Constitution, and would also uphold abortion rights (Reagan had also campaigned to make abortion illegal). Nearly

25 years later when she announced her retirement in 2005, O'Connor had earned a reputation as a pragmatic and often centrist voice as an important swing vote on issues like abortion, affirmative action, and privacy rights.[1] She remained the only woman to serve on the high court until Ruth Bader Ginsburg, appointed by President Bill Clinton, joined her in 1993.

Women's ability to lead within the judicial branch of government is somewhat different than in other political arenas. While many judges at the state level are elected, the president nominates all judges at the federal level. Judges also have distinct responsibilities and a formal process in interpreting and applying the law, as opposed to creating the laws as legislators do, which sometimes limits their ability to directly shape public policy. A good judge is also supposed to be impartial and independent, not relying on partisan or ideological viewpoints, when deciding a case. Whether or not this is true in all cases is difficult to determine; however, one would assume that a feminist judge would have a harder time changing the legal culture in America if she were staying true to her impartial judicial traditions. In terms of recruitment, judges are also not as high profile as other politicians, which makes providing female role models within the judiciary more difficult. This chapter will consider the progress women have made within the legal profession in recent decades, the history of women serving as judges at both the federal and state level, and the impact that women make on the judiciary as a whole. What is the historical relationship between women and the law in the United States? What barriers, if any, still exist for women entering the legal profession or seeking a judicial post? And, most important, do women judges make a difference in their interpretation and application of the law?

WOMEN AND THE LAW

The rule of law, which is the adherence to the basic legal foundation and rules that govern society, is fundamental to our constitutional system of government. Yet, for most of the nation's history, women did not have access to the law and the tools that it provided in shaping the political system. As we discussed in Chapter 2, not only did women lack a voice in the writing of the U.S. Constitution, women were not specifically mentioned anywhere within the document. In addition, since the founding era, the "legal status of women has been shaped by an ideology grounded in cultural and physical differences between the sexes."[2]

The legal disenfranchisement of women in American life lasted throughout the nineteenth and well into the twentieth century, despite ratification of the Fourteenth Amendment in 1868 that included clauses declaring "equal protection" and "due process" of the laws. In 1875, the U.S. Supreme Court "dismissed out-of-hand" the claim that women had a constitutional right to vote as equal citizens. Also in the late nineteenth century, the Court upheld state laws barring women from practicing law and even from working as a bartender unless the woman was a member of the owner's immediate family. These rulings only enhanced the view of women as second-class citizens. In the early twentieth century, the Court also handed down rulings, now seen as paternalistic, to protect women in the workplace regarding hours, working conditions, and wages. At the time, it was commonly assumed that women were not the equals to men in the workplace and therefore, the "problem" of women working outside the home needed to be dealt with. The Court would not begin to reverse its views of gender-based discrimination in the workplace until the early 1970s.[3]

Women were also the victims of discrimination in various other legal forms until the latter part of the twentieth century. Based on common-law traditions brought with the original American colonists from England, women lost all legal and property rights upon marriage. Married women were also denied equal custody rights, the right to keep their wages, and the right to divorce; single women also had few legal rights. Up until the early twentieth century, when many of these state laws began to be rescinded, married women were viewed as the legal property of their husbands, highlighted by a 1905 ruling by the U.S. Supreme Court that stated a husband could sue for property damages if his wife committed adultery. By losing their legal identity upon marriage, women were also banned from entering into legal contracts (which precluded them from pursuing opportunities as business owners), and they could not file a suit in a court of law.

Women were also excluded as jurors for decades after women received the right to vote in 1920, even though jury duty is considered one of the most important civic responsibilities of American citizens. Even into the 1960s and 1970s, several states granted automatic exemptions to women for jury service, which meant that states had laws excluding women as jurors. The issue was finally settled in 1975 when the U.S. Supreme Court ruled in *Taylor v. Louisiana* that excluding women violated the Sixth Amendment to the U.S. Constitution, which mandated a jury of one's peers (eliminating women did not adequately represent a cross-section of the population).

Only in recent decades have women gained access to the law as equal citizens, as a profession, and as a means to enact political changes. Spurred on by the women's movement of the 1960s and 1970s, laws (either through congressional action or rulings by the U.S. Supreme Court) finally began to reflect a woman's legal status as equal to men in the areas of property and economic rights, employment rights, and educational rights. As radical feminist and legal scholar Catharine A. MacKinnon notes:

> Law in the United States is at once a powerful medium and a medium for power. Backed by force, it is also an avenue for demand, a vector of access, an arena for contention other than the physical, a forum for voice, a mechanism for accountability, a form for authority, and an expression of norms. Women seeking change for women have found that all these consequences and possibilities cannot be left to those elite men who have traditionally dominated in and through law, shaping its structures and animating attitudes to guarantee the supremacy of men as a group over women in social life. Women who work with law have learned that, while a legal change may not always make a social change, sometimes it helps, and law *un*changed can make social change impossible.[4]

WOMEN AND THE LEGAL PROFESSION

While many career paths can lead people into a political career, a legal career—either as an attorney or judge—is a common path to elected or appointed office at the state and national levels. Women were mostly excluded from the legal profession itself until the early 1970s. Title IX of the Education Act of 1972, which guaranteed equal access to academic and athletic resources regardless of gender, dramatically increased the number of women attending law school. By 2002, women represented nearly half (49 percent) of all first-year law students in the United States[5] and 29.1 percent (more than 300,000) of all attorneys.[6] By 2004, women comprised more than 50 percent of first-year law students.

Recent studies and surveys within the legal profession have shown that women attorneys face many obstacles in achieving top leadership positions within law firms, corporations, and governmental agencies. While overt sexual discrimination may not be the biggest problem that women attorneys face in career advancement, there are organizational, institutional, and systemic obstacles that exist, including gender-based assumptions and practices, a lack of mentoring, and family–work conflicts.[7] In a recent study by the American Bar Association's Commission on Women in the Profession, women's opportunities within the legal profession, like those within the political and corporate worlds, are limited by unconscious stereotypes, inadequate access to support networks, inflexible workplace structures, sexual harassment, and bias in the justice system.[8]

Gender stereotypes are particularly problematic for women attorneys, who "often do not receive the same presumption of competence or commitment as their male colleagues."[9] A majority of women within the profession believe they are held to higher standards than men (a problem compounded for minority women). The lack of balance between work and family life also hampers career paths for women, including a double standard for working mothers who are criticized for a lack of commitment if they are not willing to sacrifice family needs for work. While no evidence exists to suggest that women attorneys with family responsibilities are any less committed to their careers, these same women are more likely to leave large law firms for a different job that offers a more flexible work schedule.[10]

Systemic gender bias within the justice system has long remained a problem for women, not only as attorneys but litigants as well. Beginning in the 1980s, several initiatives began to address some of these problems. Courts as institutions are quite traditional and formal in their practices and changes often occur slowly. For example, some courts used to sanction women attorneys who were married and refused to use their husband's last names. Whereas most cases of blatant discrimination are now rare, subtle discrimination still occurs in issues regarding the demographics of the bench (judges), bar (attorneys), and court personnel; differences in the outcomes for men and women during bail hearings or custody awards, and the general perception of participants based on gender (and also race).[11]

Most often, bias in the justice system falls into one of three categories: disrespectful treatment (for example, female attorneys being addressed by their first name while male attorneys are not, female attorneys being mistaken for support staff or being dismissed or ignored as insignificant to the proceedings); devaluation of credibility and injuries (dismissive attitudes about the importance of cases dealing with sexual harassment, employment discrimination, or acquaintance rape, for example); and stereotypical assumptions about gender, race, ethnicity, disability, and sexual orientation (domestic violence victims are somehow responsible for provoking their abuse, or that mothers who work full time are less deserving of child custody, for example). As a result, many states have implemented codes of conduct and educational programs to eliminate gender and racial bias in the courtroom.[12]

WOMEN AS FEDERAL JUDGES

Today, more than 100 courts make up the federal judicial branch. The lowest federal courts are the district courts, which serve as trial courts with juries and where most federal cases originate. If district court cases are appealed, the next step is a federal court of appeals. There are 12 federal judicial circuits (or territories), and each has its own court of appeals. With the exception of the District of Columbia, which has its own circuit, each of the other 11 circuits includes at least three states. Nine justices sit on the U.S. Supreme Court (eight associate justices and the Chief Justice), and, like other federal judges, all are appointed to life terms. Justices and federal judges can be impeached by a majority vote in the House of Representatives and removed by a two-thirds majority vote in the Senate. The latter has never happened to a Supreme Court justice, since all have served until retirement or death. When a vacancy occurs on any federal court, a potential judge or justice is first nominated for the position by the president. Next, the Senate judiciary committee considers the nomination, and if approved, it then goes to the entire Senate with confirmation occurring by a simple majority vote. Since justices and federal judges serve a life term, this is an important opportunity for presidents to enjoy a lasting political legacy long after they leave office.

When considering women appointees, however, the "integration of women into the federal judiciary has been achingly slow."[13] President Franklin D. Roosevelt appointed the first woman to a federal bench. Florence Ellinwood Allen, appointed in 1934, served on the Sixth Circuit Court of Appeals for 25 years. No other woman would be appointed to a court of appeals for 34 years, when in 1968 Lyndon Johnson nominated Shirley Ann Mount Hufstedler to the Ninth Circuit Court of Appeals (where she served until 1979). Burnita Shelton Matthews became the first woman to serve on a U.S. district court when Harry Truman issued her a recess appointment to the district court for the District of Columbia in October 1949. The Senate confirmed her nomination in April 1950. John F. Kennedy appointed one woman to a district court position, and Johnson appointed two women to district courts. Richard Nixon and Gerald Ford would appoint one woman each to a federal judgeship, both to a district court with no appointments to an appeals court.

Jimmy Carter was the first president to seriously increase the number of women serving in the judiciary, and as president, he had "both the interest and the opportunity to diversify the federal courts" in terms of gender, race, and ethnicity.[14] He appointed a total of 40 women to the federal judiciary (29 to district courts, which was 14.3 percent of his appointments, and 11, or 19.6 percent, to courts of appeals). Carter would not have the opportunity to appoint a justice to the Supreme Court during his four years in the White House, even though historically, presidents have an opportunity to make an appointment, on average, every two years. Carter's immediate successors, Ronald Reagan and George H. W. Bush, appointed fewer women to the federal bench. Reagan, who disapproved of using affirmative action policies in judicial appointments, named a total of 30 women to federal judgeships (24, or 8.3 percent to district courts and 6, or 7.2 percent, to courts of appeal). Bush appointed a total of 36 women to the federal bench (29, or 19.6 percent, to district courts and 7, or 16.7 percent, to courts of appeal).

Bill Clinton, however, reversed that trend by appointing 108 women who would serve in federal judicial posts (88, or 28.9 percent, to district courts and 20, or 30.3 percent, to courts of appeal). During his first four and a half years in office, George W. Bush has appointed a total of 44 women to the federal bench (35, or 20.5 percent to district courts and 9, or 24.3 percent, to courts of appeal; see Table 7.1). As of June 2005, a total of 43 (of 179 total positions—24 percent) women serve on federal courts of appeal and 155 (of 680 total positions—22.8 percent) women serve on federal district courts.

Historically, few women have been appointed to federal judicial positions. The main reason for the small number of women being appointed stems from the fact that up until the 1970s, so few women were entering the legal profession. So, like women seeking leadership positions within the legislative and executive branches, a limited pool of qualified women existed for presidential consideration for such posts. Bias has also existed in the selection and confirmation process. Applicants whose careers have focused on public service or public interest law are assumed to be activist on certain policy issues, which means that as judges, they go beyond merely interpreting the law to actively participate in making new law. Judicial activists can adhere to either a liberal or conservative political ideology. For example, liberal activists view the constitution as a broad grant of freedom to citizens against government interference, particularly those issues involving civil rights and civil liberties. As a result, judicial activism is sometimes viewed unfavorably during the confirmation process,

TABLE 7.1 Presidential Appointments of Women to the Federal Judiciary, 1933 to 2004 (as of June 2005)

President	District Court #Women appointments/ Total appointments	%	Appeals Court #Women appointments/ Total appointments	%	Supreme Court #Women appointments/ Total appointments	%
Franklin D. Roosevelt	0/134	0%	1/51	2.0%	0/8	0%
Harry S. Truman	1/101	1.0	0/27	0	0/4	0
Dwight D. Eisenhower	0/129	0	0/45	0	0/5	0
John F. Kennedy	1/102	1.0	0/21	0	0/2	0
Lyndon B. Johnson	2/126	1.6	1/40	2.5	0/2	0
Richard Nixon	1/181	0.6	0/46	0	0/4	0
Gerald Ford	1/50	2.0	0/11	0	0/1	0
Jimmy Carter	29/203	14.3	11/56	19.6		n/a
Ronald Reagan	24/290	8.3	6/83	7.2	1/3	33.3
George H. W. Bush	29/148	19.6	7/42	16.7	0/2	0
Bill Clinton	88/305	28.9	20/66	30.3	1/2	50
George W. Bush	35/171	20.5	9/37	24.3		n/a
Total Percentage	**205/1918**	**10.7%**	**53/519**	**10.2%**	**2/33**	**6.1%**

Sources: From the Federal Judges Biographical Database, as of June 2004.

RUTH BADER GINSBURG:

And Then There Were Two

While not as high profile as Sandra Day O'Connor's appointment to the Supreme Court in 1981, Ruth Bader Ginsburg nonetheless represented the first woman appointed to the Court by a Democrat, President Bill Clinton, in 1993. Her appointment also guaranteed that the makeup of the Court would include more than just one "woman's seat" on the bench. Ginsburg received her law degree from Columbia University in 1959 after completing her first two years of study at Harvard University. Like O'Connor, in spite of graduating at the top of her prestigious law school class (Ginsburg tied for the number one spot), Ginsburg's first job was as a legal secretary. She then received a clerkship with a U.S. district court judge, and worked for many years as a law school professor at both Rutgers University and Columbia University. She also worked as the general counsel for the American Civil Liberties Union from 1973 until 1980, when Jimmy Carter appointed her to the U.S. Court of Appeals for the District of Columbia. She served as an appellate judge for 13 years prior to her appointment to the Supreme Court in 1993.

When Clinton had his first opportunity to appoint a Supreme Court justice in 1993, Ginsburg's name appeared on the initial list of more than 40 potential candidates being considered by the White House. Ginsburg's chances for appointment were improved by a campaign waged by her husband. Unknown to Ginsburg at the time, her husband Martin worked extensively behind the scenes to garner support for her among legal scholars and those within major women's advocacy groups. Martin Ginsburg's public relations campaign helped to secure his wife's position on Clinton's short list of candidates receiving serious consideration.[15] Ginsburg also made a lasting impression on Clinton when they met prior to her nomination. Clinton was impressed by Ginsburg's family struggles (her mother died of cancer when she was 17 and her husband had also endured a battle with cancer early in their marriage) as well as her commitment to women's issues, in particular fighting gender discrimination. Clinton stated that she was the perfect candidate for the high court due to her distinguished judicial career, her advocacy work on behalf of women's issues, and her "demonstrated ability as a consensus builder [and] healer."[16]

Compared to the contentious and divisive confirmation process of Clarence Thomas in 1991 (as discussed in Chapter 5),

Ginsburg's confirmation to the Supreme Court was relatively smooth, with a 96–3 confirmation vote in the Senate. The Senate judiciary committee had also welcomed two new members in 1993—newly elected Senators Dianne Feinstein (D-CA) and Carol Moseley Braun (D-IL). Ironically, despite Ginsburg's long support of women's issues and her stance as pro-choice on the issue of abortion, several women's groups were critical of her nomination due to her belief, published within a law journal article, that the Court used the wrong rationale in its 1973 *Roe v. Wade* decision that legalized abortion. Ginsburg supported the outcome of the case, but argued that a stronger constitutional argument could have been made. This worried some pro-choice groups that she might support overturning the *Roe* decision (an outcome that has not occurred).

According to legal scholar Lawrence Baum, Ginsburg had little impact on the overall ideological balance of the conservative-leaning Rehnquist Court. Ginsburg, a moderate liberal, is similar to the justice that she replaced in terms of ideology (Associate Justice Byron White, appointed by John F. Kennedy in 1962). And, along with Stephen Breyer, a fellow moderate liberal who joined the Court in 1994, "the proportion of pro-civil liberties decisions has increased only slightly since they joined the Court, and the Court's doctrinal positions continue to be conservative in most respects."[17] Nonetheless, Ginsburg has strongly supported pro-affirmative action cases before the Court, and has also continued her fight against gender discrimination. One of her most notable majority opinions in a case came in 1996 in *United States v. Virginia*, in which the Court stated that the state-funded Virginia Military Institute's exclusion of women was unconstitutional and a violation of the equal protection clause of the Fourteenth Amendment.

Ginsburg, now in her second decade of service on the Court, has been an excellent role model for other women in the legal profession who aspire to high-ranking judicial positions. Legal scholar Lawrence Abraham gives Ginsburg high praise for her time on the Court: "Always well prepared, an articulate, incisive questioner in oral argument, a clear and often elegant writer, Ruth Bader Ginsburg has proved herself to be a genuine asset on the Court."[18] As Ginsburg herself stated at her inauguration to the Court on August 10, 1993: "A system of justice will be richer for diversity of background and experience. It will be poorer, in terms of appreciating what is at stake and the impact of its judgments, if all of its members are cast from the same mold."

particularly by those politicians who believe that judges should not seek new principles that can change the existing law, but should instead leave policymaking to elected officials. Women, particularly women of color, disproportionately come from public service backgrounds and, as a result, are often overlooked for appointments.[19]

Two other important factors have contributed to the small number of women being appointed to judicial positions. First, high standards exist in terms of education and experience for judicial office. Most candidates must not only hold a law degree, but must have several years of trial experience as well. Second, the judicial selection process is complicated and is often tied to building strong professional ties and reputations within the male-dominated legal circles. Consequently, many women do not find themselves on the short lists for consideration of these positions.[20]

WOMEN, THE COURTS, AND THE POLICY AGENDA

Women judges within the federal branch represent important political actors for women's rights. Like other areas of politics, a women's voice within judicial policymaking has the potential to bring a different perspective to the law. However, recent studies have not shown significant differences between the actions of female and male judges. Still, a diverse judiciary in terms of gender, race, and ethnicity is important for symbolic reasons. Possible explanations for the results may be the fact that so few women have served as judges, as well as the fact that gender differences may be neutralized by the act of judging, which is bound to legal traditions and processes.[21] Diversity on the bench is also important "because the federal judiciary has been arguably the most important actor in women's rights." Both reproductive rights and gender equality are "judicially created rights," since they are not specifically guaranteed in the U.S. Constitution, but have been interpreted by the Supreme Court to exist.[22] A ruling by the Supreme Court can be overturned only by a constitutional amendment or if the Court overturns itself with a new decision.

The legal system provides many institutional constraints in the exercise of power for the members of the Supreme Court. These constraints include: precedent; the parameters of constitutional and statutory law; concern for the integrity of the Court as an institution; and the decision-making process of the nine individuals who sit on the Court. Yet, as Justice O'Connor points out, having women on the bench can bring an important diversity to the selection of cases as well as the outcomes that affect policy: "None of this is to say that women do *not* differ from men in the way they exercise power, only that the differences are subtle. We all bring to the seats of power our individual experiences and values, and part of these depend on our gender."[23]

As discussed in Chapter 2, women have been viewed through the public versus private sphere dichotomy since the nation's founding. Legally, women were denied their property and their identity (separate from their fathers' or husbands'), as well as other rights as equal citizens, into the twentieth century. The judicial system, and particularly the U.S. Supreme Court, relied on "biological essentialism" to rule that women belonged only within the private sphere for nearly two hundred years before changing course in the 1970s. With several decisions dealing with women's economic rights, workplace rights, and most notably reproductive rights by the mid-1970s, the Court began to legally view women on more equal standing with men.[24] As a result, the Supreme Court, in several cases throughout the 1970s and 1980s, developed what is known as the "intermediate" or "heightened" scrutiny test to deal with gender-based discrimination. This judicial test means that any law passed that places women in a separate category from men must be substantially related to the achievement of an important government objective. As a result, the courts, and in particular the Supreme Court, have been sensitive in recent years to problems that women face in the workplace and in dealing with financial matters and have struck down certain discriminatory standards for women as unconstitutional.

WOMEN AS STATE AND LOCAL JUDGES

As part of the federal system of government, each state has its own system of courts. Whereas some states vary in the exact structure of its judicial branch, all state courts have a similar structure to the federal branch with lower trial courts, intermediate appellate courts, and a court of last appeal at the highest level (called supreme courts in most states). Only cases that deal with a federal issue can be appealed from a state supreme court to the U.S. Supreme Court. While many people believe that the federal judiciary is the most important court system in the country, in reality, nearly 95 percent of all cases are heard in state courts. The selection of judges varies in each state, with methods ranging from partisan elections (for example,

WOMEN ON THE CALIFORNIA HIGH COURT:
Ideological Diversity in Action

As the largest and most diverse state in the nation, and as a state often noted for its progressive brand of politics, it is surprising that California has yet to elect its first woman governor. However, the state's highest court cannot be criticized for having a male-dominated bench. At the start of 2005, three of the seven justices on the California Supreme Court were women. They include: Associate Justice Janice R. Brown (appointed in 1996), Associate Justice Joyce L. Kennard (appointed in 1989), and Associate Justice Kathryn Mickle Werdegar (appointed in 1994). Brown, the only African American justice on the Court, was notably more conservative than her other moderate Republican colleagues (six Republicans total), and she clashed often with moderate Chief Justice Ronald M. George. As a result, she gained the attention of the White House and President George W. Bush, who nominated her to a U.S. appellate court position in July 2003. However, Senate Democrats had successfully blocked her nomination along with certain other conservative Bush appointees to the federal bench during the first Bush term, but Brown was eventually comfirmed to the U.S. Circuit Court of Appeals for the District of Columbia in June 2005.

The most notable woman jurist in California's history, however, would have to be the state's former Supreme Court Chief Justice Rose Elizabeth Bird. As the first woman ever to serve on California's highest court upon her appointment in 1977, she served on the bench until January 1987. From the start, Bird had a distinguished career in both the law and public service. She received her law degree in 1965 from Boalt Hall School of Law at the University of California, Berkeley (a time when only a handful of women were accepted to top law schools). She clerked for the chief justice of the Nevada Supreme Court after graduation and in 1966, she became the first woman hired as a deputy public defender in Santa Clara County. She taught at Stanford Law School from 1972 to 1974, and then in 1975, Governor Jerry Brown appointed her as the first woman to serve as a cabinet member in California. As secretary of the Agriculture and Services Agency, she had administrative responsibility over 12 different state agencies.

Under Bird's leadership, the Supreme Court strengthened environmental laws, consumer rights, and the rights of women and minorities. Her accomplishments also included the 1984 adoption of the first rule to permit television and photographic coverage of court proceedings in trial and appellate courts with the consent of the presiding judge. Bird also introduced the first use of word and data processing to the Supreme Court and courts of appeal. In 1987, she appointed the Committee on Gender Bias in the courts, which began the trend for more studies in the years to follow on state courts' treatment of people based on gender, race and ethnicity, sexual preferences, and disabilities.[25]

But more important, Bird received national attention for her opposition to the death penalty, becoming a lightning rod on the issue by invalidating every one of the 58 death penalty cases that she heard on appeal. Supporters of Bird claimed that she had been "appropriately circumspect, cautious, and thorough" in her review of all 58 death penalty cases, and she was joined by at least one other justice in overturning each sentence. Opponents of Bird and her death penalty decisions claimed that she used a "series of minute legal technicalities . . . to prevent the implementation of California's death penalty" as the only California Supreme Court jurist between 1978 (when California's death penalty statute went into effect) and 1986 who had not voted to affirm a single death penalty case.[26] Bird's opponents were eventually victorious, as California voters removed Bird and two of her liberal colleagues from the Court in a 2 to 1 vote in 1986. The election marked the first time that Californians had voted not to retain a Supreme Court justice. Bird died at the age of 63 from complications of breast cancer in 1999. Since leaving the high court, she had remained completely out of the public spotlight. However, regardless of one's opinion on the death penalty, perhaps Bird's legacy can be found in the fact that California continues to have the largest backlog of death row inmates in the nation.

Texas), nonpartisan elections (for example, Oregon and Washington), or political appointment with judicial retention (for example, California, where voters decide a simple "yes" or "no" to keep a governor's choice on the bench).

In May 2003 there were 92 women justices on state courts of last resort (usually the state's supreme court) and 223 women justices on intermediate appellate courts. Twenty-eight percent of the 327 justices who served on the courts of last appeal were women, with a total of 19 women serving as the court's chief justice. Women represented 23.2 percent of the 961 justices on the intermediate appeals courts and 27 women served as the chief or presiding judge of the court.[27] In 1976, a total of 20 states had no women judges. During the Carter administration, when the president was actively appointing women and minorities to federal judicial positions, states began a similar trend. By 1979, each of the 50 states had at least one woman serving as a judge. And, between 1980 and 1991, the percentage of women state judges increased from 4 to 9 percent. By 1991, there were 14,094 judges on state courts, including 1,230 women.[28]

The increase in the number of women judges at the state level indicates a change in attitudes among voters in the states that either elect or retain judges through the ballot box. This also suggests that the eligible candidate pool for state judicial positions has broadened in many states to include the career paths of women attorneys, which can differ from that of their male colleagues (for example, more public sector work or working as a government lawyer). Of the women now serving on state courts of last resort, the demographics of this group suggest that these women are more often selected from a lower state court and also have more experience as a prosecutor than male counterparts. This trend suggests that "extensive judicial experience [may persuade] judicial selectors that non-traditional candidates are capable, despite the dissimilarity in their legal careers to more traditional white, male candidates."[29]

DO WOMEN JUDGES ACT DIFFERENTLY?

Although much more research is needed in this area to make a stronger and more definitive argument, several studies in the past three decades point to ways that women judges can not only act differently than their male colleagues, but how their presence can make a difference in the outcome of specific cases or in the shaping of public policy. An early study of how women on the bench may act differently than their male counterparts showed that in terms of convicting and sentencing, women trial judges generally did not convict and sentence felony defendants differently than men judges. However, the study of 30,000 felony cases during the time period 1971–1979 showed that men judges took a more paternalistic view toward women defendants, and women judges were twice as likely to sentence female defendants to prison than their male colleagues.[30]

Other studies since then have showed that women judges, regardless of ideology or partisan preference, tend to be stronger supporters of women's rights claims in cases than men judges, and that at least one woman serving on a bench (for example, an appeals court that hands down rulings with more than one judge participating) had a strong impact on the outcomes of sex-discrimination cases in favor of women.[31] The appointment of Sandra Day O'Connor in 1981 to the U.S. Supreme Court shifted support for women's rights on the Court, with a smaller impact coming from Ruth Bader Ginsburg's appointment in 1993. However, the two women justices have written half of the Court's majority opinions in the area of sex discrimination and serve as the Court's "spokespeople" for women's rights issues.[32] Some feminist scholars have also looked for what is considered to be a "different" or "feminist" voice in legal decisions emanating from women judges. Little evidence exists to date that would show that placing women on the bench has altered modes of legal reasoning throughout the judiciary. Yet, with much more work to be done in terms of researching the impact of women judges as they continue to move beyond token status, as well as increasing the number of women nominees to judicial positions, "real changes in the law have been, and will continue to be, the result of the hard work done by women in the American judiciary."[33]

CONCLUSION

As with other political institutions, women are just now starting to make an impact in terms of their representation as judges at all levels of the judicial system. While it may be too early to tell if women judges will dramatically change the processes and outcomes of the judiciary's role in policymaking at both the state and national level, it is clear that women continue to enter the legal profession in record numbers and will no doubt continue to gain many more judicial positions in the coming years. According to Sandra Day O'Connor, her role, along with colleague Ruth Bader Ginsburg, as the only two women on the Supreme Court has been to serve as important role models for other women aspiring to top leadership positions: "My intuition and my experience persuade me that having women on the bench, and in other positions of prominence, is extremely important. The self-perception of women is informed by such examples, and by the belief of women that they, too, can achieve professional success at the highest levels."[34]

The appointments of O'Connor and Ginsburg, according to Lawrence Baum, "reflect changes in society that made it at least somewhat less difficult for people other than white men to achieve high positions." As we have seen in recent years, presidents are now more willing to consider women and members of racial minority groups as judicial nominees. But, "Because of the various advantages they enjoy, white men are [still] more likely to enjoy disproportionate representation on the Court for some time."[35] That dominance within the legal profession, however, is not nearly as strong as it once was as women continue to break down barriers to achieve positions of power and leadership within the federal and state judicial branches.

STUDY/DISCUSSION QUESTIONS

1. What progress have women made in the legal profession in the latter part of the twentieth century? Why has this been so important for women entering judicial positions at both the state and federal level?
2. Why have women experienced difficulty in achieving presidential appointment to judicial positions at the federal level?
3. How have Sandra Day O'Connor and Ruth Bader Ginsburg made a difference for women in the legal profession with their service on the U.S. Supreme Court?
4. What role have women played within state court systems in recent years?
5. How might women judges have an impact on public policies affecting women?

SUGGESTED READINGS

Baer, Judith A. 1999. *Our Lives Before the Law: Constructing a Feminist Jurisprudence.* Princeton: Princeton University Press.

Goldstein, Leslie Friedman, ed. 1992. *Feminist Jurisprudence: The Difference Debate*. Lanham, MD: Rowman Littlefield.

Lyles, Kevin. 1997. *The Gatekeepers: Federal District Courts in the Political Process*. Westport, CT: Praeger.

Mezey, Susan Gluck. 1992. *In Pursuit of Equality: Women, Public Policy, and the Federal Courts*. New York: St. Martin's Press.

Mezey, Susan Gluck. 2003. *Elusive Equality: Women's Rights, Public Policy, and the Law*. Boulder, CO: Lynne Rienner.

O'Connor, Sandra Day. 2003. *The Majesty of the Law: Reflections of a Supreme Court Justice*. New York: Random House.

Rhode, Deborah L. 2001. *The Unfinished Agenda: Women and the Legal Profession*. ABA Commission on Women in the Profession.

ONLINE RESOURCES

http://www.nawj.org/news.html. National Association of Women Judges.

http://www.law.stanford.edu/library/wlhbp. Women's Legal History Biography Project.

http://www.ncwba.org/History.html. National Conference of Women's Bar Associations.

http://www.fjc.gov/history/home.nsf. Federal Judges Biographical Database, Federal Judicial Center.

NOTES

1. Biography of Sandra Day O'Connor, Oyez, U.S. Supreme Court Multimedia, accessed at http://www.oyez.org/oyez/resource/legal_entity/102/biography.
2. Susan Gluck Mezey, *In Pursuit of Equality: Women, Public Policy, and the Federal Courts* (New York: St. Martin's Press, 1992), 8.
3. See Mezey, *In Pursuit of Equality*, 10–17; and David M. O'Brien, *Constitutional Law and Politics*, vol. 2, *Civil Rights and Civil Liberties*, 5th ed. (New York: W.W. Norton, 2003), 1475.
4. Catharine A. MacKinnon, "Women and Law: The Power to Change," in *Sisterhood Is Forever: The Women's Anthology for a New Millennium*, ed. Robin Morgan, 447 (New York: Washington Square Press, 2003).

5. Legal Education Statistics Fall Enrollment 2002. American Bar Association Section of Legal Education and Admission to the Bar. Quoted in "A Current Glance at Women in the Law 2003," accessed at http://www.abanet.org/women/glance2003.pdf.

6. National Lawyer Population Survey Statistics 2003. American Bar Association Marketing Research Department. Quoted in "A Current Glance at Women in the Law 2003," accessed at http://www.abanet.org/women/glance2003.pdf.

7. Jacob H. Herring, "Can They Do It? Can Law Firms, Corporate Counsel Departments, and Governmental Agencies Create a Level Playing Field for Women Attorneys?" in *The Difference "Difference" Makes: Women and Leadership,* ed. Deborah L. Rhode, 76 (Stanford, CA: Stanford University Press, 2003).

8. Deborah L. Rhode, "The Unfinished Agenda: Women and the Legal Profession," ABA Commission on Women in the Profession, 2001, 5.

9. Ibid., 6.

10. Ibid., 7.

11. Ibid., 20.

12. Ibid., 20–22.

13. Barbara Palmer, "Women in the American Judiciary: Their Influence and Impact," *Women & Politics* 23, no. 3 (2001): 95.

14. Richard L. Pacelle Jr., "A President's Legacy: Gender and Appointment to the Federal Courts," in *The Other Elites: Women, Politics, and Power in the Executive Branch,* ed. MaryAnne Borrelli and Janet M. Martin, 154 (Boulder, CO: Lynne Rienner, 1997).

15. Lawrence Baum, *The Supreme Court,* 8th ed. (Washington, DC: Congressional Quarterly Press, 2004), 34.

16. Henry J. Abraham, *Justices, Presidents, and Senators: A History of the U.S. Supreme Court Appointments from Washington to Clinton* (Lanham, MD: Rowman & Littlefield, 1999), 318.

17. Baum, *The Supreme Court,* 135.

18. Abraham, *Justices, Presidents, and Senators,* 322.

19. Rhode, "The Unfinished Agenda," 26.

20. Elaine Martin, "Women Judges: The New Generation," in *Women in Politics: Outsiders or Insiders?* ed. Lois Duke Whitaker, 278 (Upper Saddle River, NJ: Prentice Hall, 1999).

21. Kevin L. Lyles, *The Gatekeepers: Federal District Courts in the Political Process* (Westport, CT: Praeger, 1997), 262–63.

22. Pacelle, "A President's Legacy," 149.

23. Sandra Day O'Connor, *The Majesty of the Law: Reflections of a Supreme Court Justice* (New York: Random House, 2003), 195.

24. Sue Thomas, *How Women Legislate* (New York: Oxford University Press, 1994), 18–20.
25. "Chief Justice Rose Elizabeth Bird Dies; Supreme Court to Hold Memorial Session," News Release of the California Supreme Court, December 6, 1999, No. 78, accessed at http://www.courtinfo.ca.gov/presscenter/newsreleases/NR78-99.HTM.
26. "The Death Penalty," accessed at http://www.rosebirdprocon.org/.
27. "Women Justices Serving on State Courts of Last Resort and Intermediate Appellate Courts, 2002," National Center for State Courts, accessed at http://www.gendergap.com/governme.htm.
28. Barbara A. Curran and Clara N. Carson, *The Lawyer Statistical Report: The U.S. Legal Profession in the 1990s* (Chicago: American Bar Foundation, 1994), accessed at http://www.gendergap.com/governme.htm.
29. Martin, "Women Judges," 283–84.
30. John Gruhl, Cassis Spohn, and Susan Welch, "Women as Policy-makers: The Case of Trial Judges," *American Journal of Political Science* 25, no. 2 (May 1981): 308–22.
31. For example, see Sue Davis, Susan Haire, and Donald Songer, "Voting Behavior and Gender on the U.S. Courts of Appeal," *Judicature* 77 (1993): 129–33; Elaine Martin, "The Representative Role of Women Judges," *Judicature* 77 (1993): 166–73; and Gerard Gryski, Eleanor Main, and William Dixon, "Models of State High Court Decision Making in Sex Discrimination Cases," *Journal of Politics* 48 (1986): 143–55.
32. Barbara Palmer, "Justice Ruth Bader Ginsburg and the Supreme Court's Reaction to Its Second Female Member," *Women & Politics* 24, no. 1 (2002): 1–23.
33. Barbara Palmer, "Women in the American Judiciary: Their Influence and Impact," *Women & Politics* 23, no. 3 (2001): 89–99.
34. O'Connor, *The Majesty of the Law,* 189.
35. Baum, *The Supreme Court,* 58.

Conclusion: Women and Political Leadership in the Twenty-first Century

A woman will be president. Why? Because we're expert cleaners and the world is a mess.

—Marie Wilson
founder of the White House Project

*T*he role of women in American public life presents both a long and complex story and a work in progress. For all of the gains made in terms of public policies changed, offices held, and barriers broken, many challenges remain for women political leaders on both ends of the political spectrum. As stated in Chapter 1, those with political power are those who hold specific leadership positions within government. Even though we can imagine how different the political process might look and operate if all government officials were women, the reality remains that at the start of the twenty-first century, women are still nowhere near holding even half the seats of power at all levels of the American government. Achieving that goal may be possible, but slower progress in the last few years in placing women into political leadership positions suggests that it may take longer than talked about just a few years ago in 1992, The Year of the Woman. In this concluding chapter, we will briefly consider future challenges for women within the political process as voters, candidates, and political officeholders. Returning to the theme of leadership, we will also consider how women impact the political and policymaking process as leaders and what the future may hold.

THE WOMEN'S MOVEMENT

As we discussed in Chapter 2, a third wave of the women's movement has emerged that looks somewhat different than its predecessor yet still represents some basic themes of feminism and legal equality. However, there is disagreement within feminist circles about what a third wave of the women's movement stands for or even if it truly exists. For the most part, this younger generation of feminist activists is pursuing a more global and inclusive perspective than did the second wave of the women's movement to include a much wider range of women's views and relevant issues. Perhaps the biggest challenge for the leaders of this current movement is simply the political environment in which they find themselves attempting to pursue certain policies. The current focus of governmental resources on foreign policy issues related to terrorism and national security has left little room on the U.S. policy agenda, or within the national political dialogue, for feminist voices to be heard. And with a more complex and broader definition of feminism and women's rights than during the second wave of the women's movement, there is no clear consensus on which to build an agenda. According to historian Barbara Epstein, "The wind has gone out of the sails, not only of the women's movement but also of the progressive movement as a whole in the United States generally. . . . Part of the answer is that feminism has become more an idea than a movement. And even as a movement, it lacks some of the impetus that it once had."[1]

Nonetheless, legal reform within the American governing system is still seen by many women's rights activists as a top priority. Legal scholar Susan Gluck Mezey argues that legal reform can serve as an important vehicle for effecting societal change, and while the law by itself cannot end "political, social, and economic inequality, it sets a standard and creates a tone, in no small part because it responds to and helps engender awareness of feminist goals."[2] In recent decades, the fight for legal equality based on gender through the court system was in large part a success for women's rights activists as they gained many new legal rights in the areas of work, education, and economic issues. However, pay equity, the lack of women at higher levels of corporate and government leadership, attempts to restrict reproductive freedom, and the lack of effort to integrate family responsibilities for both women and men with their jobs are still important problems that persist within our society. As Mezey concludes, law and politics are "not perfect methods for transforming the United States into a more egalitarian society. Thus despite important achievements in the law, society is not at the point where the differences between the sexes are interesting and intriguing but not determinative of a person's rights and stature."[3]

VOTING TRENDS AND THE GENDER GAP

Women make up more than half of the voting population in the United States and during each election have the potential to make or break any particular candidate. Women have also had higher voter turnout than men in recent elections. Yet, whereas women may be seen as "the crown jewel of the electorate,"[4] the gender gap has narrowed in recent presidential elections as women are increasingly divided over key political issues. Given that women have never represented a monolithic voting bloc to begin with, that should not surprise any political observer. During the 2004 presidential election, the complexities of how women vote became even more apparent. The 2004 election showed there is a widening gulf between married women, who tend to vote Republican, and single women, who tend to vote Democratic. Democrats increased turnout among single women, while Republicans helped secure George W. Bush's reelection victory with the aid of married women voters in strong Republican states in the Midwest and the South. However, in spite of the increasing marriage gap among both female and male voters, many political experts agree that the overall gender gap is "alive and well and cuts across marital, racial and age lines."[5]

In 2004, Democrats appeared to have fallen short by their failure to rally women over their strongest issues, including health care and economic security, losing ground among white, working, and married women. The abortion issue also continues to play an important role in party politics, with each party struggling to define itself on the divisive issue. The Republican Party currently faces the challenge of contending with various factions within its ranks, which include moderates (who may be fiscally conservative but socially moderate and pro-choice), the old right (fiscal conservatives who favor small government and are mostly pro-life), and the new right (social conservatives who are staunchly pro-life and support government intervention in areas such as morals and social values). The Democrats, after their electoral losses in 2004, are debating whether or not to distance themselves from their long-standing position of being pro-choice because of the Republican Party's success with voters on issues such as family and morality. At the start of the 109th Session of Congress in 2005, Democrats selected a new Senate minority leader, Harry Reid of Nevada, who happens to be pro-life. Just a few years ago, placing a pro-life politician in a top leadership position within the Democratic Party would have been unheard of; as recently as 1992, the party refused to allow William Casey, then-Democratic governor of Pennsylvania, a speaking role at the Democratic National Convention due to his pro-life stance. But in the current political environment—and having lost the last two presidential elections and being out of control of both houses of Congress simultaneously since 1995—some within the party see Reid's ascension to Senate minority leader as a moderating move to tone down the abortion rhetoric to not alienate those voters who lean more toward the middle of the political spectrum. How this issue will play out within the political arena in regard to women voters remains to be seen, yet both parties seem committed in their attempts to increase voter registration and turnout among women.

WOMEN AS CANDIDATES

As discussed in Chapter 4, in spite of the progress that women candidates have made in the area of campaign finance and the ability to raise adequate funds to run a successful campaign, many barriers remain to keep women from running for or getting elected to public office. The power of incumbency presents the biggest challenge, since this provides such a large advantage to holding onto a political office. Because most incumbents are men, that makes it harder for women to break into the political realm since they are still viewed as the "other" in the electoral arena. Also, women candidates need more encouragement to run, not only from individual supporters but from parties and interest groups as well. Making the decision to run for political office is often the largest hurdle for a woman candidate to overcome. While public opinion polls show that American voters largely support women both as active participants in the political process and as candidates, recent studies also suggest that many women still believe they will have a difficult time winning an election. This may be due to continuing stereotypes of women candidates and the emphasis on a difference that they represent. According to political scientist Kathleen Dolan, "We still, in journalistic, popular, and academic accounts of their activities, refer to them as 'women candidates.' That we modify the noun 'candidates' in this way indicates that candidate sex is still a relevant, or at least obvious, aspect of their electoral activities."[6]

We do know that women voters do not automatically vote for women candidates, and that party identification and incumbency can play a much larger role than the gender of the candidate in terms of voter preference.[7] However, the number of women seeking elective office has leveled off in recent years, with fewer women running for state legislative positions in 2004. Since political experience is often an important qualification for seeking higher political office, such as a state governor or member of Congress, the decline for women seeking state-level lesiglative positions is not a positive trend. The recruitment of women into political careers, as well as breaking down pervasive stereotypes about women candidates, becomes even more important because many political observers believe that the importance of national security issues and "continued perceptions among some voters as well as some potential female candidates that women should be caring for their families have limited participation."[8]

WOMEN AS OFFICEHOLDERS

In recent years, several studies have shown that women officeholders, especially in both Congress and state legislatures, do make a difference in policy outcomes, particularly in those policies directly affecting women.[9] At the start of 2005, a total of 14 women were members of the U.S. Senate, and while a rate of 14 percent may still be low, several of those women on both sides of the political aisle are either high-profile members (for example, Hillary Rodham Clinton, D-NY; and Elizabeth Dole, R-NC) or have gained tremendous ground in terms of seniority and committee assignments (for example, Barbara Mikulski, D-MD; Dianne Feinstein, D-CA; Barbara Boxer, D-CA; Olympia Snowe, R-ME; and Kay Bailey Hutchison, R-TX).

In the House of Representatives, the Congressional Caucus for Women's Issues faces many challenges in the next few years, including the recruitment of reliable co-chairs from each party (Republican "feminists" are sometimes hard to recruit and it is difficult for them to commit to the agenda); recruiting enough reliable and committed members from each party; maintaining organizational structure that promotes the agenda (without the same staffing that the caucus had enjoyed in the past, holding regular meetings and reaching consensus among the growing membership has become more difficult); finding a usable agenda that is streamlined and focused on obtainable goals; adjusting to competing claims on national resources (the increased attention on terrorism, national security, and military and defense funding makes budgetary concerns for women's issues more challenging); and connecting with the White House and congressional leaders (the caucus's relationship with the administration of George W. Bush has been distant, and women's or feminist issues are not prioritized on the conservative Republican agenda). However, the urgency of domestic issues such as Social Security in the next few years suggests that the caucus will continue. As congressional scholar Irwin Gertzog argues, the caucus "is among the more long-lived informal groups in the House. Its robust size, its elastic agenda, its faithful membership, and its attentive constituency suggest that the organization will probably carry on for a while."[10]

The question also still remains as to when a woman will be elected president or vice president. Public opinion polls continue to show overwhelming support among voters for a women to be elected president, yet there seems to be a continuing disconnect between that sentiment and the reality of presidential electoral politics. Our system of presidential nominations is often a contest of "the survival of the fittest" in terms of money, party support, name recognition, and a positive public image. Potential women contenders are already on the public's short list for 2008, including Hillary Rodham Clinton, Elizabeth Dole, and Condoleezza Rice.[11] Yet, time will tell if any or all of these women, or others as well, choose to run for the White House and, perhaps more important, survive the primary process long enough to at least let voters determine their fate in the earliest primary contests.

Regardless of when the political glass ceiling is broken at the national level, both political parties must recognize that all women politicians, whether legislators or governors, bring a unique experience to government and policymaking. What political scientist Kim Fridkin Kahn pointed out a decade ago is still true today, that "by limiting the number of women in elective office, we limit the attention of the government to predominantly male concerns and ignore the concerns of women and women legislators. A governing body that neglects a range of issues not only ignores the concerns of a large segment of the electorate but also may be less effective than a government addressing a wider spectrum of policy concerns."[12]

CONCLUSION:
WOMEN AND LEADERSHIP REVISITED

As this book illustrates, there is no universal definition for leadership, particularly in regard to women in the political arena. Defining successful leadership is an elusive task, and the debate will continue regarding the role that gender can play in better understanding the notion of leadership and the difference that it can make in the political process. According to political scientist Sue Thomas, "leadership can be exerted in a wide variety of ways, informally and formally, and in a multiple milieus." The fact that leadership may also be a gendered concept has "implications for the possibilities and constraints on women in both achieving leadership positions and the ways they act once those positions are gained." As a result, she suggests that future academic studies of women and political leadership should move beyond the narrow view of only those who hold formal positions of political power to include women of varying racial or ethnic and socioeconomic backgrounds who are active political participants, as well as leaders in the political process in formal positions at all levels of government (elected and appointed positions); other political positions such as lobbyists and staff assistants; and informal (civic, community, business, and church organizations) positions.[13] Expanding our view of how women can alter policy outcomes in a variety of leadership positions will provide a better understanding of the role of women in our society, past, present, and future.

Women as political leaders in American life have made much progress since the Seneca Falls Convention in 1848, yet much work remains as today's leaders forge ahead into the twenty-first century. Whether in the political and legal arenas, the corporate world, higher education, or any number of important civic or social roles, women leaders can bring different perspectives to public life and can continue to help break down negative cultural stereotypes about women in our society. Many barriers to equality for women have been broken down with the help of the election and appointment of women to high-ranking political positions. More women will have access to these positions of power as our society continues to accept and embrace women as political leaders. Women, when viewed as an inclusive group, represent political perspectives, policy choices, and backgrounds that run the gamut of partisan and ideological preferences. However, if the level of political participation of its citizens defines the level of democracy within a government, then the continued increase of all women as active political participants will help ensure that the democratic ideal of our system of government will endure.

STUDY/DISCUSSION QUESTIONS

1. What are some of the challenges that the women's movement will face in the next decade? Will the third wave of the women's movement be successful?
2. Will the gender gap in voting continue, and what are the prospects for increasing voter turnout among women?
3. What are the biggest challenges that women candidates continue to face in the electoral arena? What are some suggestions for increasing the number of women running for public office?
4. Will women ever reach parity with men in terms of elected and appointed political positions at the state and national levels?

NOTES

1. Barbara Epstein, "The Successes and Failures of Feminism," *Journal of Women's History* 14, no. 2 (June 2002): 118.
2. Susan Gluck Mezey, *Elusive Equality: Women's Rights, Public Policy, and the Law* (Boulder, CO: Lynne Rienner, 2003), 3.
3. Ibid., 288.
4. Eleanor Clift, "Capitol Letter: The Gender Gap," *Newsweek,* May 14, 2004.
5. Lynn Sweet, "Did the Women's Vote Count?" *Chicago Sun-Times,* November 10, 2004, p. 60.
6. Kathleen Dolan, *Voting for Women: How the Public Evaluates Women Candidates* (Boulder, CO: Westview Press, 2004), 153.
7. Ibid., 156.
8. Susan Milligan, "Regression After Year of the Woman," *Boston Globe,* January 30, 2005, p. A14.
9. See Amy Caiazza, "Does Women's Representation in Elected Office Lead to Women-Friendly Policy? Analysis of State-Level Data," *Women & Politics* 26, no. 1 (2004): 35–65.
10. Irwin N. Gertzog, *Women and Power on Capitol Hill: Reconstructing the Congressional Women's Caucus* (Boulder, CO: Lynne Rienner, 2004), 161.
11. Marc Humbert, "Poll: 6 in 10 Ready for U.S. Woman Leader," *Associated Press,* February 22, 2005.

12. Kim Fridkin Kahn, *The Political Consequences of Being a Woman* (New York: Columbia University Press, 1996), 138.

13. Sue Thomas, "The Impact of Women in Political Leadership Positions," in *Women and American Politics: New Questions, New Directions,* ed. Susan J. Carroll (New York: Oxford University Press, 2003), 89–90.

Index

AAUW, 56, 59
Abortion, 26, 53, 57
Abraham, Lawrence, 137
Accuracy in Media, 77
Adams, Abigail, 17
Adams, John, 17
Advancing Women, 124
AERA, 18–19
Aggregative (transactional) leadership, 5, 82
Aiken, George, 110
Albright, Madeleine, 2, 112, 113, 114
Allen, Florence Ellinwood, 133
American Association of University Women (AAUW), 56, 59
American Equal Rights Association (AERA), 18–19
American Woman Suffrage Association (AWSA), 19
American Women Presidents, 123
Anthony, Susan B., 15, 18, 19, 22–23
Antisuffrage movement, 19
Aquino, Corazon, 6
Arneil, Barbara, 32
Ashcroft, John, 83
Attorneys, 131–132
AWSA, 19

Backlash: The Undeclared War on American Women (Faludi), 27
Barnes, Kay, 121
Baum, Lawrence, 137, 144
Baumgardner, Jennifer, 31
Bayless, Betsey, 119
Beauty Myth: How Images of Beauty Are Used Against Women, The (Wolf), 27
Bender, Jane, 121
Bentsen, Lloyd, 86
Bernstein, Carl, 48
Biographical sketches
  Anthony, Susan B., 22–23
  California High Court, 140–141
  Ferraro, Geraldine, 72–74
  Gandy, Kim, 54–55
  Ginsburg, Ruth Bader, 136–137
  Graham, Katherine, 48–49

Pelosi, Nancy, 92–93
  presidential contenders, 110–111
  Sanchez, Loretta, 88–89
  Stanton, Elizabeth Cady, 22, 23
  Steinem, Gloria, 28–29
Biological essentialism, 139
Bird, Rose Elizabeth, 140–141
Black feminism, 34
Blyth, Myrna, 46
Bono, Mary, 83
Bono, Sonny, 83
Book, Esther Wachs, 104
Book, overview, 9–12
Bourque, Susan C., 4
Boxer, Barbara, 69, 85, 86, 87, 152
BPW, 56
Braden, Maria, 71
Breyer, Stephen, 137
Brown, Janice R., 140
Brown, Jerry, 140
Brownmiller, Susan, 26
Bundling, 69
Burns, James MacGregor, 5
Bush, Barbara, 116
Bush, George H. W., 112, 134, 135
Bush, George W., 40, 47, 49, 93, 108, 112, 113, 134, 135, 140, 150
Bush, Laura, 47, 116
Business and Professional Women (BPW), 56
Business careers, 105

Caballero, Anna M., 121
Cabinet appointments, 112–114
Cable TV, 46
California High Court, 140–141
campaign financing, 68–70
Campbell, Jane, 4, 120, 121
Candidate recruitment, 63–66
Candidates. *See* Political candidates
Cannon, Martha Hughes, 95
Cantwell, Maria, 87
Capsule biographies. *See* Biographical sketches
Caraway, Hattie Wyatt, 83
Carnahan, Jean, 83

Carnahan, Mel, 83
Carroll, Susan J., 65, 67
Carsey, Marcy, 104
Carter, Jimmy, 53, 108, 134, 135
Carter, Rosalyn, 116, 117
Casey, William, 151
Catt, Carrie Chapman, 20, 56
Center for Media and Public Affairs, 77
Chao, Elaine, 113, 114
Chapman, Carrie, 56
Chicana feminism, 34
Chisholm, Shirley, 110
Clinton, Bill, 31, 108, 112, 134–136
Clinton, Hillary Rodham, 87, 109,
    116–118, 152, 153
Colby, Bainbridge, 20
Collins, Susan, 87
Command-and-control style, 104
Commission on the Status of Women
    (1961), 26, 53
Concerned Women for America (CWA),
    26, 56
Congress, 86, 87, 90
Congressional Caucus for Women's Issues,
    90–91, 152–153
Cosmopolitan, 46
Costain, Anne N., 16
Cressingham, Clara, 95
Criminal justice system, 128–147
    actions of women judges, 142–143
    anti-female bias, 132–133
    California High Court, 140–141
    federal judges, 133–138
    Ginsburg, Ruth Bader, 136–137
    legal constraints, 130
    state/local judges, 139–142
    women attorneys, 131–132
Crossfire, 74
Cultural attitudes, 42–43
CWA, 26, 56

D'Alesandro, Thomas J., Jr., 93
Dateline, 46
Davis, Gray, 89
"Declaration of Sentiments and
    Resolutions" (Stanton), 18
DeGeneres, Ellen, 46
Democratic Party
    abortion, 150–151
    current situation, 150

EMILY's List, 57
    women voters, 40
    women's issues, 31, 52–53
Disenfranchisement, 130. See also
    Suffrage movement
Dissenting leadership, 22
Dolan, Kathleen A., 43, 151
Dole, Elizabeth, 70, 71, 87, 102, 109, 111,
    112, 114, 152, 153
Doman, Robert, 88
Dr. Phil, 47
Dunn, Irina, 29

Eagle Forum, 21, 26, 56
Early money, 69
Ecofeminism, 35
Eisenhower, Dwight D., 135
Eisenhower, Mamie, 116
Electoral realignment (1980), 50
EMILY's List, 69
Epstein, Barbara, 149
Equal Pay Act, 26
Equal Rights Amendment (ERA), 21, 24,
    26, 53
Evans, Pat, 121
Evans, Sara M., 32
Executive leadership, 102–127
    business careers, 105
    cabinet appointments, 112–114
    first lady, 116–117
    governors, 118–119
    mayors, 120–122
    new paradigm leaders, 104–105
    on-deck circle, 108
    presidential candidates/contenders,
        102, 110–111
    statewide positions, 120
    vice-president, 109
    White House advisors, 115–116
    women president, 106–112

Faludi, Susan, 27
Fargo, Heather, 121
FECA, 68
Federal Election Campaign Act
    (FECA), 68
Federalist 10, 51
Feinstein, Dianne, 69, 80, 86, 87,
    137, 152
Felton, Rebecca Latimer, 83

Feminine Mystique, The (Friedman), 24–25
Feminism, 31–35. *See also* Women's movement
  defined, 32
  eco, 35
  gender, 35
  global, 35
  liberal, 32
  Marxist-socialist, 33
  postmodern, 34–35
  psychoanalytical, 35
  radical, 33
  women of color, 33–34
Feminist Majority Foundation, 37
Ferguson, Miriam "Ma," 3, 119
Ferraro, Geraldine, 62, 71, 72–74, 84
Ferraro: My Story (Ferraro), 73
Fiorina, Carleton S. "Carly," 105
First Ladies Gallery, 124
First lady, 116–117
Flores, Elizabeth G., 121
Ford, Gerald, 53, 109, 133, 135
48 Hours, 46
Fourteenth Amendment, 130
Franking, 66
Franklin, Barbara, 114
Franklin, Shirley, 120, 121
Freeman, Jo, 52
Friedan, Betty, 24–25, 54
Fundraising, 68–70

Gandy, Kim, 54–55
Gender feminism, 35
Gender gap, 47–51, 109
Gender-specific work, 75
Gender stereotyping, 132. *See also* Stereotyping
Generation X feminists, 30
George, Ronald M., 140
Gephardt, Richard, 93
Gertzog, Irwin, 153
Ginsburg, Martin, 136
Ginsburg, Ruth Bader, 3, 129, 136–137, 144
Glamour, 46
Global feminism, 35
Good Housekeeping, 46
Good Morning America, 46
Governors, 118–119
Graham, Katherine, 48–49

Graham, Philip, 48
Grasso, Ella, 3, 119

Hardy, Jill, 121
Harmon, Jane, 69
Harris, Patricia Roberts, 114
Hart, Gary, 111
Heckler, Margaret, 114
Heightened scrutiny test, 139
Helgesen, Sally, 102
Henry, Astrid, 27, 30
Herman, Alexis, 114
Hill-Thomas controversy, 86–87
Hills, Carla Anderson, 3, 114
Hobby, Oveta Culp, 2, 114
Holly, Carrie C., 95
Holmes-Norton, Eleanor, 85
Holtzman, Elizabeth, 74
Homemaker individual retirement account, 7
House of Representatives, 87, 90
Huffington, Michael, 69
Hufstedler, Shirley Ann Mount, 114, 133
Hughes, Karen, 3, 115, 116
Hull, Jane Dee, 119
Hutchison, Kay Bailey, 7, 86, 87, 152

In-depth coverage. *See* Biographical sketches
Incumbency advantage, 66–68
Independent Women's Forum, 56
Inner cabinet, 112–113
Institute for Women's Leadership, 124
Integrative (transformational) leadership, 5, 82
Interest groups, 55–57
Intermediate scrutiny test, 139
Iorio, Pam, 121
Ireland, Patricia, 54
Isaac, Teresa, 121

Johnson, Ladybird, 116
Johnson, Lyndon, 133, 135
Journalism. *See* Mass media
Judiciary/judges. *See* Criminal justice system
Jurors, 130

Kahn, Kim Fridkin, 70, 153
Kassebaum, Nancy, 85
Keegan, Lisa Graham, 119

Kellerman, Barbara, 2
Kennard, Joyce L., 140
Kennedy, Flo, 26
Kennedy, John F., 25, 53, 107, 133
Kerry, John, 40, 47, 119
Kerry, Teresa Heinz, 47
Klock, Frances, 95
Kreps, Juanita, 114

Ladies' Home Journal, 46
LaHaye, Beverly, 26
Landes, Bertha K., 120
Landrieu, Mary, 87
Latina feminism, 34
Leadership, 154
    executive. *See* Executive leadership
    gender differences, 6–7
    legislative, 81–82
    styles of, 5, 82
    women, 4
League of Women Voters (LMV), 20, 56
Legal profession. *See* Criminal justice
    system
Legislative leadership, 81–82
Legislators, 80–101, 152–153
    Congress, 86, 87, 9086–87
    *Congressional Caucus for Women's
       Issues,* 90–91, 152–153
    Hill-Thomas controversy, 86–87
    historical overview, 82–87
    House of Representatives, 87, 90
    leadership, 81–82
    Pelosi, Nancy, 92–93
    Sanchez, Loretta, 88–89
    Senate, 87, 90
    state legislatures, 91–97
    widows, 83
Liberal feminism, 32
Lieberman, Joseph, 107
Lifetime, 46
Lincoln, Blanche, 87
Lipstick watch, 71
Live With Regis and Kelly, 47
LMV, 20, 56
Local judges, 139–142
Locke, John, 32
Lockwood, Belva, 110

MacKinnon, Catharine A., 131
Madison, James, 51

Magazines, 46
Male-female differences
    communication, 8
    judges, 142–143
    leadership styles, 6–7
Mandel, Ruth B., 43, 63–64
Manross, Mary, 121
Mansbridge, Jane J., 24
Marriage gap, 49
Martin, Lynn, 114
Marx, Karl, 33
Marxist-socialist feminism, 33
Mass media, 43–47, 43–47. *See also*
    Mass media
    gender-specific work, 75
    lipstick watch, 71
    magazines, 46
    negative stereotyping, 44–45, 70, 71
    talk shows, 46
    theories, 43–44
    trivialization of women, 8, 70, 75
    TV, 46
    women political candidates, 70–75
    women working in, 45–46
    women's appearance, 71, 75
Matsui, Doris, 83
Matsui, Robert, 83
Matthews, Burnita Shelton, 133
Mayors, 120–122
McLaughlin, Ann, 114
McLin, Rhine L., 121
Mecham, Evan, 119
Media. *See* Mass media
Media systems dependency approach, 44
Meyer, Eugene, 48
Mezey, Susan Gluck, 149
Michaels Debra, 31
Mikulski, Barbara, 7, 84, 85, 87, 152
Mill, John Stuart, 32
Miller, Laura, 4, 120–121, 121
Minimal effects approach, 43–44
Mink, Patsy, 85
Miroff, Bruce, 22
Mitchell, George, 85
Mofford, Rose, 119
Mondale, Walter, 71, 72
Money (campaign financing), 68–70
Mormon Church, 21
Moseley Braun, Carol, 55, 86, 102, 111, 137
Mott, Lucretia, 17, 22

Multicultural feminism, 35
Murkowski, Lisa, 87
Murphy Brown, 30
Murray, Patty, 86, 87
Myers, Dee Dee, 3, 115

Napolitano, Janet, 119
National American Woman Suffrage
    Association (NAWSA), 20
National Association of Women
    Judges, 145
National Conference of Women's Bar
    Associations, 145
National Consumer's League, 19
National Council of Catholic Women, 21
National Organization for Women
    (NOW), 25, 54, 56
National Woman Suffrage Association, 23
National Women's History Project, 37
National Women's Political Caucus, 56
NAWSA, 20
Negative stereotyping, 8, 44–45, 70, 71
Network TV, 46
Neustadt, Richard, 7
New paradigm leaders, 104–105
News media. *See* Mass media
Nineteenth Amendment, 19
Nixon, Richard, 48, 53, 133, 135
Nolan, Mae Ella, 92
Norris, Pippa, 50
Norton, Gale, 113, 114
NOW, 25, 54, 56
NOW/PAC, 55

Oberndorf, Meyera E., 121
O'Connor, Sandra Day, 3, 128–129, 138,
    143–144
O'Donnell, Rosie, 46
Officeholders. *See* Legislators
O'Leary, Hazel, 114
On-deck circle, 108
O'Neill, Beverly, 121
O'Neill, Tip, 73
Online resources
    executive leadership, 123–124
    feminism, 37
    generally, 12
    judiciary/legal profession, 145
    legislature, 99
    media, 77

political candidates, 77
political participation, 59
women's movement, 37
Open-seat elections, 67, 68
OpenSecrets.org, 77
Orr, Kay A., 119
Outrageous Acts and Everyday Rebellions
    (Steinem), 28
Outsider strategy, 108
Oxygen, 46

PAC, 56–57, 69
Paletz, David L., 44
Parents, 42
Paul, Alice, 18, 20, 21
Peer groups, 42
Pelosi, Nancy, 3, 80, 92–93
Pentagon Papers case, 49
Perkins, Frances, 2, 3, 112, 114
Perot, H. Ross, 103
Personal History (Graham), 49
Physical appearance, 71, 75
Places Where Women Made History, 37
Plan of the book, 9–12
Political action committee (PAC),
    56–57, 69
Political activism, 51–57
Political candidates, 62–79, 151–152
    early money, 69
    eligibility, 65
    Ferraro, 72–74
    fundraising, 68–70
    incumbency advantage, 66–68
    media coverage, 70–75. *See also*
        Mass media
    money (campaign financing), 68–70
    open-seat elections, 67, 68
    physical appearance, 71, 75
    recruiting women candidates, 63–66
Political participation, 40–61, 150–151
    cultural attitudes, 42–43
    gender gap, 47–51
    interest groups, 55–57
    marriage gap, 49
    mass media, 43–47. *See also* Mass media
    PACs, 56–57, 69
    political activism, 51–57
    political parties, 51–54
    political socialization, 41–43
    voting, 47–51

Political parties, 51–54. *See also* Democratic Party; Republican Party
Political power, 7
Political socialization, 41–43
Postfeminism, 30
Postmodern feminism, 34–35
Powell, Colin, 107
President, 103, 106–112
President's Commission on the Status of Women (1961), 26, 53
Presidential cabinet, 112–114
Presidential candidates/contenders, 102, 110–111
Presidential election (2004), 40
Primetime, 46
Prominent women. *See* Biographical sketches
Psychoanalytic feminism, 35

Radical feminism, 33
Radical-cultural feminism, 33
Radical-libertarian feminism, 33
Rankin, Jeannette, 83
Reagan, Ronald, 53, 72, 108, 112, 128, 134, 135
Redbook, 46
Redistricting, 67
Reid, Harry, 151
Reno, Janet, 2, 114
Republican Party
  current situation, 150
  ERA, 53
  factions, 150
  family and mortality, 151
  WISH List, 57
  women's issues, 31, 53
Revolution, 23
Revolution from Within: a Book of Self-Esteem (Steinem), 28
Rice, Condoleezza, 2, 3, 109, 113, 114, 115, 153
Richards, Amy, 31
Richards, Ann, 119
Roe v. Wade, 26
Roosevelt, Eleanor, 116, 117
Roosevelt, Franklin D., 133, 135
Roseanne, 30
Rosen, Ruth, 26
Rosenthal, Cindy Simon, 81–82
Ross, Jim Buck, 74

Ross, Nellie Tayloe, 3, 119
Rule of law, 129

Safe seats, 67
Salter, Susanna, 120
Sanbonmatsu, Kira, 53, 65
Sanchez, Loretta, 88–89
Schlafly, Phyllis, 21, 26
Schroeder, Patricia, 84, 85, 102, 111
Schumer, Charles, 74
Scruggs, Elaine M., 121
Seltzer, Richard A., 50
Senate, 87, 90
Seneca Falls Convention, 17–18
Seng, Coleen, 121
Shalala, Donna, 114
Slaughter, Louise, 85
Smeal, Eleanor, 50, 54
Smith, Margaret Chase, 110
Snowe, Olympia, 7, 87, 90, 152
Spellings, Margaret, 114
Spencer, Loretta, 121
Spin sisters, 46
Springer, Carol, 119
Stabenow, Debbie, 87
Stanton, Elizabeth Cady, 18, 19, 22, 23
Stanton, Henry, 22
State legislatures, 91–97
State/local judges, 139–142
Statewide positions, 120
Stealth feminists, 30
Steinem, Gloria, 26, 28–29
Stereotyping, 8, 44–45, 70, 71, 132
Suffrage movement, 18–20
Susan B. Anthony House, 37
Susan B. Anthony List, 57, 69
Symbolic annihilation, 8, 70

Talk shows, 46
Taylor v. Louisiana, 130
Television, 8, 46
Thatcher, Margaret, 6
Thelma & Louise, 30
Third Wave Foundation, 37
Thomas, Clarence, 86
Thomas, Sue, 154
Thomas-Hill controversy, 86–87
Title IX of the Education Act of 1972, 26, 131
Today Show, The, 46

Transactional leadership, 5, 82
Transformational leadership, 5, 82
Trivialization of women, 8, 70, 75
Truman, Harry, 133, 135
TV, 8, 46
Two-income family, 26
20/20, 46

United States v. Virginia, 137
Unsoeld, Jolene, 85
Uses and gratifications approach, 44

Valles, Judith, 121
Veneman, Ann, 113, 114
Vice president, 109
View, The, 47
Voter turnout, 41
Voting, 47–51. *See also* Political
      participation

Washington insider *vs.* outsider
      phenomenon, 108
Washington Post, The, 48
Watergate scandal, 48
Wattleton, Faye, 1
Web sites. *See* Online resources
Werdegar, Kathryn Mickle, 140
White, Byron, 137
White House advisors, 115–116
White House Project, 71, 105
Whitman, Christine Todd, 40, 113
Whitman, Meg, 104
Why the Best Man for the Job Is a Woman
      (Book), 104
Widows, 83
Will, George, 73
Wilson, Edith, 116
Wilson, Marie, 105, 148
Wilson, Woodrow, 20
Winfrey, Oprah, 46
WISH List, 69
Wolf, Naomi, 27
Woman's Day, 46

Women president, 106–112
Women's Campaign Fund, 57
Women's Equity Action League, 56
Women's Legal History Biography
      Project, 145
Women's Loyal National League, 23
Women's magazines, 46
Women's movement, 15–39, 149–150.
      See also Feminism
   abortion, 26
   Anthony, 22–23
   antisuffrage movement, 19
   Backlash, 27
   Beauty Myth, 27
   Equal Pay Act, 26
   ERA, 21, 24, 26
   Feminine Mystique, 24–25
   first wave, 16–24
   origin, 17–18
   postsuffrage era, 20
   Roe v. Wade, 26
   second wave, 24–27
   Stanton, 22, 23
   Steinem, 28–29
   suffrage movement, 18–20
   third wave, 27–31
   Title IX, 26
Women's Policy, Inc., 99
Women's Trade Union League, 19
Women's Voices, Women's Vote, 47, 59
Woodhull, Victoria, 110
Woodward, Bob, 48
Workingwoman's Association, 23
World Anti-Slavery Convention
      (1840), 18

Yard, Molly, 54
Year of the Angry White Male (1994), 76
Year of the Woman (1992), 68, 86

Zaccaro, John, 72
Zuckerman, Mort, 28